THE CRITICS DEBATE

General Editor Michael Scott

SONS AND LOVERS

Geoffrey Harvey

MACMILLAN

For Nicholas and Michael

First published 1987

Published by
Higher and Further Education Division
MACMILLAN PUBLISHERS LTD
Houndmills, Basingstoke, Hampshire RG21 2XS
and London
Companies and representatives
throughout the world

Printed in Hong Kong

Harvey, Geoffrey
D.H. Lawrence, Sons and Lovers. – (The Critics debate)
1. Lawrence, D.H. Sons and lovers
I. Title II. Series
823'.912 PR6023.A9356

ISBN 0–333–37954–3
ISBN 0–333–37955–1 Pbk

Contents

General Editor's Preface

OVER THE last few years the practice of literary criticism has become hotly debated. Methods developed earlier in the century and before have been attacked and the word 'crisis' has been drawn upon to describe the present condition of English Studies. That such a debate is taking place is a sign of the subject discipline's health. Some would hold that the situation necessitates a radical alternative approach which naturally implies a 'crisis situation'. Others would respond that to employ such terms is to precipitate or construct a false position. The debate continues but it is not the first. 'New Criticism' acquired its title because it attempted something fresh calling into question certain practices of the past. Yet the practices it attacked were not entirely lost or negated by the new critics. One factor becomes clear: English Studies is a pluralistic discipline.

What are students coming to advanced work in English for the first time to make of all this debate and controversy? They are in danger of being overwhelmed by the cross curents of critical approached as they take up their study of literature. The purpose of this series is to help delineate various critical approaches to specific literary texts. Its authors are from a variety of critical schools and have approached their task in a flexible manner. Their aim is to help the reader come to terms with the variety of criticism and to introduce him or her to further reading on the subject and to a fuller evaluation of a particular text by illustrating the way it has been approached in a number of contexts. In the first part of the book a critical survey is given of some of the major ways the text has been appraised. This is done sometimes in a thematic manner, sometimes according to various 'schools' or 'approaches'. In the second part the authors provide their own appraisals of the text from their stated critical standpoint, allowing the reader the knowledge of their own particular approaches from which their views may in turn be evaluated. The series therein hopes to introduce and to elucidate criticism of authors and texts being studied and to encourage participation as the critics debate.

Michael Scott

A Note on Text and References

QUOTATIONS from *Sons and Lovers* are taken from the Penguin English Library edition, edited with an introduction and notes by Keith Sagar (Harmondsworth, 1981), as being the text and most readily available to the reader.

Several of the critical essays referred to in this book are included in *D.H. Lawrence, 'Sons and Lovers': A Casebook*, edited by Gámini Salgádo (London: 1969), from which quotations are taken for the convenience of the reader, who may wish to consult this volume. Other works cited are identified by author and year of publication; full details will be found in the Reference section.

Introduction

ALTHOUGH the publication of *Sons and Lovers* marked Lawrence's emergence as a major novelist, as R.P. Draper has noted [1969], we do not know how many copies were originally printed. But the sales of the first edition were apparently somewhat disappointing, and a second edition did not appear until 1922. By the 1930s, however, it had become the most popular of all Lawrence's novels. Its initial reception was generally favourable, but a number of critics felt that Lawrence had not worked sufficiently hard at the novel's form, even though, as Lawrence had written to Edward Garnett, who edited *Sons and Lovers* for the publisher, Duckworth, he had taken considerable pains with its form, and had paid particularly close attention to achieving the organic unity necessary in a novel concerned with the process of growing-up. Several critics also objected to the disturbing eroticism of some aspects of the novel, and indeed some of Garnett's suggested cuts in the text may have been made on the grounds of their sexual content. Some of the more perceptive critics found *Sons and Lovers* arresting because of its powerful realism – the way it evokes almost tangibly the atmosphere of English industrial working-class life, its introduction of an unheroic central character, and its sheer power to surprise with its immediacy and truth. Few early critics did justice to its thematic and formal complexity, however. Indeed, several of them misread the novel altogether, casting the plucky Mrs Morel as its heroine and treating Paul's relationship with his mother as representing the normal loving support given by a son, who is forced by circumstances to assume his shiftless father's domestic role. However, the *avant garde* intellectuals, prompted by professional psychoanalysts, who took a keen interest in this novel, drew attention to a very different interpretation inspired by the psychoanalysis of Sigmund Freud – then very much in vogue – that the intense mutual love of mother and son is abnormal and essentially destructive, a view which still dominates critical discussion of the novel.

In writing this survey of *Sons and Lovers* criticism, together with my own appraisal of the novel, I have tried to produce the kind of book which I should have found helpful as a student. Today it seems to be even more necessary, for over recent years not only have there been several important developments in literary criticism and critical theory, but there has emerged what is generally felt to be a crisis in English studies – not simply about what critical approaches to English literature are most fruitful, but about what actually constitutes English literature itself – which has intensified the whole atmosphere of critical debate. The latter issue, which has been discussed recently in books by Peter Widdowson [1982] and Terry Eagleton [1983], is strictly beyond the scope of this study, but the flurry of activity in literary criticism has meant, from the student's point of view, an increase in the number of competing ideologies and critical voices, which in the case of a central author such as D.H. Lawrence and a major novel such as *Sons and Lovers* may appear confusing and even daunting. From a negative point of view, critics may be regarded as combative and contradictory, always at odds with one another without ever arriving at a definitive interpretation of a text. Put more positively, the variety of sharply conflicting views of *Sons and Lovers* is testimony to its profundity. It refuses to be reduced to a single discursive statement. Moreover, because the act of critical interpretation involves in some degree a response only not of the individual reader's ideological orientation, but also of his moral imagination, it can never be reduced to orthodoxy. Also students will recognise that, while every critic has the right to his opinion, critical views and procedures are not all of equal merit, and, to the extent that students assess the inequality of value among the critical essays they are reading, their own critical faculty is being sharpened. It is one of the aims of this book to foster that process.

In Part One, the survey of critical approaches, I have been constrained by my sense of what is most useful and also by practicalities. Thus, for instance, structuralist, linguistic or deconstructionist interpretations of *Sons and Lovers* are not included because they are judged to be less helpful to students than other more popular views competing for space in this book. It follows that I have chosen criticism which focuses on interpreting the text, rather than criticism which employs the text as the basis for a philosophical debate which leads into the more rarified areas of critical theory. Although the majority of the critics chosen represent the best in Lawrence criticism, they have ben selected primarily because they belong to particular identifiable and well-established schools of criticism, which students will come across in their study of *Sons and Lovers*. These schools I have designated 'source criticism', 'psychoanalytical criticism', historical criticism', 'feminist criticism', 'formalist criticism' and 'genre criticism'. However, I should make it clear that these are convenient umbrella terms. For instance, by formalist criticism I do not mean the school that developed out of Russian formalism, nor specifically American New Criticism; rather I am employing the term in the broader sense of criticism which has approached the study of *Sons and Lovers* through an examination of its formal components, or structure, with the aim of revealing how this embodies Lawrence's imaginative vision and the novel's meaning. Moreover, it will become apparent that some of these terms shall be treated cautiously; for instance, historical criticism is frequently based on a Marxist view of history, and is sometimes referred to as Marxist Criticism! Finally, some of the critics discussed as members of a particular school could be considered with some justification as belonging to another; for instance, one of my examples of feminist criticism is also essentially historical in its approach, while genre analysis is clearly concerned with the novel in its formal aspect.

It will become clear what precisely is involved in each of these critical approaches, but this is an appropriate point to indicate some of my principles of selection. Great novels such as *Sons and Lovers*, because of the profundity of their ideas and art, attract a variety of critical approaches. Because much of the story of Paul and the Moral family was based on Lawrence's own experience, the novel has interested those critics who are concerned with investigating the source of fiction in the writer's own life and with the external influences that are brought to bear on the novel through the various stages of its writing. Lawrence had already produced a draft of the novel – at that stage a melodrama set in a middle-class milieu – when at the instigation of Jessie Chambers (the model for Miriam Leivers) he re-wrote it and gave instead a fictionalised account for his own childhood and growth to maturity. Similarly, *Sons and Lovers* is also peculiarly open to the clinical probing of psychoanalytical criticism, which reads the novel as the revelation of the operation of Lawrence's unconscious, discerning in it a classic case-study of Freud's famous Oedipus complex.

Historical critics, on the other hand, focus on the fact that Lawrence was the son of a Nottinghamshire coal-miner and that *Sons and Lovers* is the first English novel to deal with working-class life in an industrial community from the inside. This criticism, which is more clearly ideological in its orientation, offers an analysis of Lawrence's treatment of an industrial, capitalist society. However, a high degree of politcal commitment is also evident in feminist criticism, which approaches *Sons and Lovers* from the point of view of Lawrence's representation of women. This school of criticism, which regards issues of gender as of paramount importance, tends to identify with the novel's women and is mainly hostile to Lawrence.

The largest and most inclusive school, formalist criticism, which was the dominant critical approach in the middle years of this century and which is still influential, considers the way the novelist has organised and objectified his imaginative response to life in the structural patterns of his fiction. Formalism may be narrowly defined, by its interest in the novel's patterns of symbolism, for instance; or it may be concerned with narrative structures in a broadly schematic way; or it may offer a more flexible interpretation of the novel's artistic complexity and its rhetoric. This general approach has links with the final school which I discuss, the more limited, yet in some ways broader, concerns of genre criticism, which sees *Sons and Lovers* as possessing the well-defined pattern belonging to genres which deal with the education of the child through adolescence to adulthood, and often in particular concern themselves with the development of the artist. This approach considers *Sons and Lovers* therefore in terms of its affinity with a range of English and European fiction.

In Part Two, the appraisal section, I develop my own estimation of *Sons and Lovers*, explaining why I regard a critical approach combining elements of liberal humanism and formalism as the most flexible method of revealing the nature and quality of Lawrence's art in this novel. Although I find much of value in each of the schools of criticism discussed in the survey, I try to move beyond their limited points of view in my appraisal. Essentially, in examing the novel's formal elements, I am concerned to make out a case for regarding *Sons and Lovers*, more positively than critics have tended to, as a consciously crafted work, rather than the passive vehicle for Lawrence's unconscious, his inspirational vitalism, or his deterministic historical realism. I emphasise therefore his deliberate endeavour to transcend the constraints of autobiography, and through his marvellous control of the narrative point of view to sustain a high degree of artistic impersonality. I also stress his successful achievement of an organic unity in this novel, and the way in which he employs the novelist's craft in his interweaving of elements from both drama and poetry into its intricate form. Because for Lawrence the truth about any human situation was extremely complex, its multi-faceted nature is embodied in the formal density of *Sons and Lovers*, and it is this overwhelming commitment to human truth and to the truth of his art which makes *Sons and Lovers* one of his finest novels.

PART ONE: SURVEY

Source criticism

THE GENESIS of *Sons and Lovers* is well known. It is possible to trace the influence of two women on the composition of the novel: Jessie Chambers, on whom Miriam was modelled, and Frieda Lawrence, who helped Lawrence in the later stages of the writing. More than most novels, therefore, *Sons and Lovers* offers, through an examination of its sources, an insight into the nature of Lawrence's creativity. One of the basic sources is Jessie Chambers's own account of its origins [1935]. The novel was two-thirds written when Lawrence first showed it to her and she noted the sense of strain in its 'extremely tired writing' and its 'story-bookish quality' [*Casebook*, p.41]. It possessed a conventional bourgeois setting, in which Miriam was the daughter of a middle-class shopkeeper, and a melodramatic plot, in which Mr Morel killed his son, Arthur, with a carving-knife during a row, and died soon after his release from prison. Jessie Chambers felt that Lawrence's own life was more poignant and interesting than his novel, particularly that part of it which was represented by the strenuous opposition of Paul's mother to his love for Miriam, which Jessie immediately identified as its central theme and which, she believed, 'if treated adequately, had in it the stuff of a magnificent story' [*Casebook*, p.42].

Jessie provided Lawrence with notes of her recollections of their friendship, but, although she admired the realism and sympathy evident in the revised manuscript which Lawrence showed her, she was bewildered and dismayed at his treatment of their relationship in the story of Paul and Miriam. It lacked any acknowledgement of their warm sympathy and of her years of devotion to his genius, and she commented bitterly that Lawrence's mother 'had to be supreme, and for the sake of that supremacy every disloyalty was permissible' [*Casebook*, p.45]. Although at Lawrence's urging Jessie tried to overcome her sense of betrayal by reminding herself that it was only a novel, she was unable to disentangle fiction from life. Indeed, for her the wholly fictional elements are an intrusion, confirming her feeling about Lawrence's psychological and moral failure: 'The events related had no foundation in fact, whatever their psychological significance. Having utterly failed to come to grips with his problem in real life, he created the imaginary Clara as a compensation' [*Casebook*, pp. 45–6].

In his discussion of 'The Miriam Papers' (Jessie's notes and her comments on the manuscript) Harry T. Moore [1964] indicates the nature and extent of Jessie's contribution to the novel's genesis. Although Lawrence incorporated several of her episodes, she was in no sense a collaborator, for he improved her notes and transmuted her rather ordinary account of their youthful experiences, making the individual episodes contribute to the novel as an artistic whole. From her comments on the manuscript, it is clear that her disagreement with Lawrence's treatment of the Paul and Miriam section focused in particular on her sense that, in transposing their experience into fiction, Lawrence fails to realise the purity of Miriam's love, stresses unfairly her inability to comprehend Paul, and obscures Paul's incapacity to experience spiritual as well as sexual love. Above all, however, Jessie blamed Paul and Mrs Morel for their complicity in Miriam's defeat.

Jessie Chambers's vigorous response has stimulated a critical debate about the issue of Lawrence's artistic honesty in this novel. A.H. Gomme, for instance, states that 'the question for the critical reader is not whether Lawrence is being fair to Jessie Chambers, but whether he is honest about Miriam Leivers' [1978, p.37]. For Gomme this issue hinges on Lawrence's consistent adoption of Paul's point of view, which reflects his mother's dominant will and which overrides the objective, dramatic presentation of Miriam's own words, and he concludes, 'Paul's tragedy is the corruption of spontaneous life in the service of an inflexible ideal, Lawrence's and Jessie's in the impossibility of self-detachment from the forces which make the idea all-powerful' [p.49].

Frieda Lawrence's influence on the gestation of *Sons and Lovers* has been examined by Frederick J. Hoffman [1953] and

Graham Hough [1956]. Hoffman is particularly concerned with her Freudianism. One of her close friends had been a disciple of Freud and when she first encountered Lawrence, she records in a letter to Hoffman, they discussed Freud's theories. Indeed, Hough quotes her own comment that on the day of their first meeting she and Lawrence 'talked about Oedipus and understanding leaped through our words' [p.55], which serves to confirm that, although Lawrence later remarked that he had not read Freud when he was engaged in writing *Sons and Lovers*, he was certainly familiar with Freud's central theory of the Oedipus complex. Like Jessie, Frieda at once identified the mother–son theme as the novel's centre, but in Freudian terms, as she wrote in a letter to Edward Garnett: 'I think L. quite missed the point in *Paul Morel*. He really loved his mother more than anybody, even with his other women, real love, sort of Oedipus' [*Casebook*, p.28]. And Graham Hough agrees with Frederick Hoffman that Lawrence's discussions with Frieda about Freud, while he worked on the final version of the novel, may have resulted in enhancing the already prominent mother–son relationship. However, this point should not be stressed unduly because, as Hoffman points out, *Sons and Lovers* contains no explicit clinical or psychological commentary (indeed, Lawrence was suspicious of Freud's clinical view of sexuality) and in any case, as Lawrence himself was well aware, the Oedipal situation was there in the autobiographical reality on which he drew. As Jessie Chambers told her friend Helen Corke, Lawrence made it clear to her after his mother's death what was the nature of the obstacle between them: 'I've loved her – like a lover – that's why I could never love you' [quoted Hough, 1956, p.55].

One of the fullest accounts of the source material of *Sons and Lovers* is given by John Worthen [1979], who detects the existence of several versions of the novel during the two years Lawrence was engaged in writing it. Worthen argues that, since the first version was begun around October 1910, when his mother was ill, Lawrence's natural tendency would be to eulogise his mother and revile his father. This story went into a second version in March 1911, to be called *Paul Morel*, which Jessie Chambers saw, and the result of her assistance, according to Worthen, was a further version which was 'not simply the tragedy of a brutal, even murderous father, and a wronged mother, but the tragedy of a damaged child' [p.33]. This was the version, written in the spring of 1911, which she regarded as a treachery: Lawrence had glorified his mother, made Paul a painter (thus omitting the literary and intellectual discussions between Lawrence and Jessie) and made Miriam, by all accounts, a less impressive figure than Jessie Chambers. However, in spite of her protest, Lawrence left the Miriam sections virtually unaltered. Following Frederick Hoffman, John Worthen points out (citing Lawrence's statements in a letter to Rachel Annand Taylor in December 1910, that he loved his mother like a husband – *Casebook*, p.22) that the idea of the existence of an Oedipal relationship between Paul and his mother had been in his mind since the very beginning of *Sons and Lovers*, and that therefore Frieda's influence on the final version, commenced in September 1912, lay in her confirmation for Lawrence that the core of the novel was indeed Freudian. The result was that in the final text the mother became the dominant figure, a decision which Worthen regards as confirmed by Lawrence's summary of the novel that he sent to Garnett (discussed below in the section on psychoanalytical criticism), in which he insists that the concentration on the mother imparts formal coherence to the novel.

The central argument in John Worthen's account of the novel's origins lies in his explanation of the change of title from *Paul Morel* to *Sons and Lovers*, a decision made under the impact of Lawrence's new idea of Paul being caught between Miriam and his mother; and in his view this alteration of the novel, influenced by Freudianism, marred certain aspects of the book. It precluded the sort of love that could interfere with Paul's Oedipal feelings, and it made the rejection of Miriam more complicated. Moreover, it led Lawrence in his summary of the novel to Garnett to misinterpret William's death in terms of a Freudian 'split' between his mother and Lily. Similarly, John Worthen argues, Paul's affair with Clara is ended abruptly in order to make room for the more important event of Mrs Morel's death and Paul's response to it. And finally, says Worthen, in adopting the idea that came to him in the autumn of 1912, Lawrence had to 'weaken the book's characteristic strength: its creation of the Morel family understood not simply in psychological or moral terms, but as it existed in a community' [p.42].

Criticism which derives from the study of the source of *Sons and Lovers* allows us a privileged glimpse into the nature of Lawrence's creativity and into his response to criticism, discussion and assistance from Jessie Chambers and Frieda Lawrence. Jessie Chambers's account reveals how badly Lawrence needed her prompting to make the break with conventional fiction, to embark on his realistic study of life in a mining community and to transmute his own experience into fiction. However, her record fails in the end to make the crucial distinction between life and art, and it concerns itself too much with the strictly irrelevant question of whether Lawrence treated her fairly. Harry T. Moore offers an insight into Lawrence's transformation of Jessie's notes, and also into her disagreement with the way he turned the historical truth of their friendship into a very different truth of fiction; while arguing from the basis of Jessie's experience, A.H. Gomme feels that Miriam's defeat is artistically dishonest because Lawrence loads the narrative point of view against her, which is the result of Lawrence's inability to gain artistic detachment from his material – a view which rests on a strictly limited reading of the novel's form.

Other critics, however, look to the influence of Frieda rather than Jessie, particularly Frederick Hoffman, Graham Hough and John Worthen. They are all agreed that Lawrence was aware of the Freudian dimension of his novel, but that his later discussions with Frieda confirmed and deepened this understanding. Worthen, however, goes further. His discussion of the way that, under the influence of the two women closest to him, Lawrence first recast conventional melodrama into social realism, and then modified the novel in accordance with the demands of the Freudian pattern, is valuable. And it is clear from the evidence I have considered that something like this took place. But Worthen's attempt to tease out the conscious and unconscious strands in Lawrence's creative endeavour is sometimes unbalanced. For instance, Lawrence makes it clear that Paul's break with Clara is slow and tortured rather than abrupt, and that it takes place for reasons that have relatively little to do with his Oedipus complex. Moreover, Paul's adolescence, education and job in Nottingham make his growing away from the tightly knit community of Bestwood inevitable and appropriate. Essentially, Worthen's argument depends on the weight he gives to the tyranny over Lawrence's imagination of the idea of the Oedipus complex, which intruded late into the process of the novel's creation and resulted in a changed thematic focus halfway through, with a consequent disruption of its form. However, it is clear from Lawrence's letters, as well as from the novel itself, that the Oedipal element is there from the beginning and is worked through in the text with great consistency. The fundamental weakness of this critical approach, which is shared by those critics who discuss Jessie Chambers's contribution and response to *Sons and Lovers* as well as by those who focus on Frieda Lawrence's influence, is an inability to break free of biography and to accord Lawrence a proper degree of artistic detachment and control over the form and meaning of the novel.

Psychoanalytical criticism

Psychoanalysis was developed in the late nineteenth century by Sigmund Freud as a method of studying the growth of the human personality. In particular he was interested in the function of sexuality within that process. Freud's theory regarded the Oedipus complex as constituting the relations essential to our development into social beings; but he also employed it to explain breakdowns in the normal pattern of sexual and emotional development. Essentially, it is a mechanism for effecting the transition from childhood to mature independence, enabling the adult to engage in a network of social relations. In the case of a boy, his early intimate involvement with his mother's body produces an unconscious incestuous desire, which also in effect casts his father in the role of his rival. However, through fear of castration, the boy represses this desire into his unconscious, submits to his father, casts himself off from his mother and identifies more and more with his father, who comes to symbolise his own future manhood. If the Oedipus complex is not successfully overcome in this way, however, the boy may become fixated on his mother, and in Freud's view this may lead either to an inability to form proper sexual relationships with women, or to homosexuality.

At the time Lawrence was writing *Sons and Lovers* the intellectual *avant garde* had already taken up Freud, and when it was published they immediately sought to explain the psychological development of both Paul Morel and Lawrence himself in Freudian terms. They were encouraged in this line of interpretation by Lawrence's decision to alter the title from *Paul Morel*, which implied a traditional, picaresque novel with a central protagonist, to *Sons and Lovers*, which seemed to place the emphasis on a series of sexual relationships with the mother at the centre. Indeed, Lawrence himself gave a Freudian account of the novel in a letter to Edward Garnett, in which he describes how the mother selects her sons as lovers, urging them into life, but produces in them as a result a crippling inability to love other women and a hatred of their father. The 'split' between his mother and a rival woman kills William, and when the same 'split' appears in Paul Mrs Morel realises what is the matter and begins to die, leaving Paul at the end, says Lawrence, 'naked of everything with the drift towards death' [*Casebook*, p.25].

Much to Lawrence's amusement and pleasure, not only the intelligentsia of the day, but professional psychoanalysts as well, came to regard *Sons and Lovers* as the most profound examination in literature of the workings of the Oedipus complex, and as an artistic corroboration of the scientific truths revealed by Freud's method of analysis. One of the earliest psychoanalytical interpretations was made by Alfred Booth Kuttner [1916] in an essay which in its essentials has effectively not been superseded. Although Kuttner regards *Sons and Lovers* highly as literature, he values it chiefly for 'the support it gives to the scientific study of human motives' [*Casebook*, p.69], and in particular to Freud's theory of the Oedipus complex. His argument rests on the assumption that the novel's Oedipal pattern has not been imposed consciously by Lawrence; rather, the novel is 'built up internally . . . out of the psychic conflicts of the author, and any testimony which it may bear to the truth of the theory involved will therefore be first hand' [*Casebook*, p.70]. In support of his thesis Kuttner points to Lawrence's preoccupation with the identical theme of mother–son relationships in early poems such as 'End of Another Home Holiday' [*Casebook*, pp.52–4], and early plays and novels such as *The Widowing of Mrs Holroyd* and *The White Peacock*, in which a guilty love between son and mother and hatred between son and father play an important part.

As befits a scientific investigation, Alfred Kuttner works in a methodical, detailed way. First he demonstrates how Mrs Morel's guilt at having given birth to Paul out of a loveless relationship impels her to lavish all her affection on him; how they are bound up with one another emotionally; how with her middle-class values she aesthetises him; and how all this leads to his refusal of ordinary boyhood. Kuttner argues that Paul's effeminacy reverses the normal pattern of courtship between him and Miriam, and that further strain is placed on their relationship by Mrs Morel, whom Kuttner regards as a jealous vampire figure, clinging to Paul as her substitute husband. Torn between the two women, Paul spiritualises his relationship with Miriam and later returns to his mother, regressing in the process into a childlike attitude to life, in which his only desire is to live in peaceful solitude with an eternally youthful mother. Perceiving this impulse to be suicidal, Mrs Morel encourages Paul's safer relationship with Clara Dawes, who succeeds in removing Paul's sexual inhibitions, but finds that he can only love her impersonally, thus undermining their love affair. Realising that his mother is destroying his life's happiness, Paul wishes for her death, but discovers afterwards that he can live neither with her nor without her, and that in death she simply creates a permanent, ideal union between them.

Alfred Kuttner then proceeds to measure his condensed account of Paul's emotional life against his straightforward description of Freud's theory of the Oedipus complex, very similar in essence to the outline given above. He is particularly concerned to emphasise the inhibiting effect on mature sexual relations of circumstances which force a child into a specialised attitude towards either parent. Applying a Freudian analysis to *Sons and Lovers* with great acuteness, Kuttner sees the novel as offering a pattern of both normal and abnormal behaviour. Although we all have something of Paul in us, we can see clearly in him 'the tremendous role that the abnormal fixation upon the parent plays in the psychic development of the individual' [*Casebook*, p.87]. In Paul's case this is conditioned by his father's unnatural position in the family, and by his mother's unusually intense love for him. Paul can never make the sexual and emotional transfer away from his mother, and the result is emotional paralysis. Moreover, the mechanism of repression never operates to release him from these deeply disturbing feelings for his mother and father, because he is never free of the incubus of his parents long enough to develop his own sense of selfhood.

I have given Alfred Kuttner's analysis at some length because it illustrates some of the strengths and limitations of his early analytic approach to *Sons and Lovers*. One of its virtues is its lucid exposition of the clear parallels between Lawrence's life, Paul Morel's development and Freud's Oedipus complex. It offers an illuminating insight into Lawrence's creative inner life. But it should be treated with caution. Echoing Lawrence's own statement in a letter to A.W. McLeod that 'one sheds one's sickness in books' [*Casebook*, p.26], Kuttner sees the novel as therapeutic both for Lawrence and his readers, and this view of the novel as therapy is far removed from considering the novel as art. Because for Kuttner the novel's scientific value lies in its revelation of the workings of the unconscious, he reads it as a straightforward transcription from life, denying Lawrence any real artistic control over his material. Kuttner's approach is therefore reductive in making no distinction between art and life, in seeing Paul Morel primarily as a case-history, and in regarding Lawrence the artist as little more than a medium for psychological theory. Moreover, his essay is too narrowly based on the mother–son theme, because, by concentrating on the universal implications of the psychoanalytic theory embodied in the novel, he omits to attend to those social and historical contexts within which Paul Morel also has his development. Lawrence may have been pointing to this kind of limitation and distortion when he said in a letter to Barbara Low that Kuttner's article had reduced the 'fairly complete truth' of his art in *Sons and Lovers* to a 'half lie' [*Casebook*, p.27].

Later exponents of the psychoanalytical method of criticism offer a subtler interpretation of the Freudian pattern in this novel. Daniel A. Weiss [1962] discovers a greater degree of complexity in the son–lover relationship, by identifying Paul Morel's need to retain a faith in his mother's purity out of an unconscious jealousy of his father. Yet Paul's Oedipal drive requires both purity and incest, and in this respect, argues

Weiss, Miriam and Clara, Paul's alternative choices, also represent a composite mother figure. Miriam is the 'virginal madonna', whom he finally shakes loose as a mother surrogate and replaces by Clara Dawes, a harlot figure who, as Daniel Weiss points out (quoting Freud in support of his argument) is the opposite of Mrs Morel and Miriam, and with whom he is enabled finally to make the incestuous identification with his mother. However, as with Miriam, in his relationship with Clara Paul's sexuality is essentially passive, regressive and deathlike. Nevertheless, because both relationships are 'determined by the root Oedipal relationship', says Weiss [p.43], Miriam and Clara are finally released from their function as mother surrogates by Mrs Morel's death.

Another area in which Daniel Weiss extends Kuttner's analysis is in his discussion of the combined functions of Clara and Baxter Dawes. In doing so he draws on Freud's theory that Oedipal man needs an 'injured third party'; that is, he requires his chosen woman to be someone else's possession. Moreover, he needs her to be in some way sexually discredited, so as to correspond with his debased and cynical view of his mother's sexual relations with his father. From this point of view, Baxter Dawes functions in a more complex way as a father figure, so that, by transferring his Oedipal feelings to this parallel set of relations, Paul is able to act out his incestuous desires with his mother surrogate at the same time as injuring his 'father'; and he can achieve both with impunity.

Daniel Weiss stresses even more than Kuttner the importance of Mrs Morel in Paul's development, although in his view Paul's Oedipal hatred for his father is modified by his growing identification with Baxter Dawes and by the concomitant decline in the vitality of the mother surrogates. However, for Weiss the conclusion of the novel embodies Paul's rejection of all the elements of his Oedipal involvement, and an acceptance of his father's values. Because Paul refuses death and is finally initiated into the world of manhood through his decision to turn back towards the town, *Sons and Lovers*, Weiss argues, is not a tragedy but rather a 'comedy of the Oedipus complex' [p.65]. However, Paul's choice of a positive solution carries relatively little conviction in Weiss's presentation of it, because the whole burden of his argument is that Paul inhabits a highly deterministic world of neurotic paralysis. Moreover, although Weiss's essay is full of subtle insights, like Kuttner's it views the author as a psychological medium, having minimal control over the selection of his material. He reads the novel as the recorded psychology of its author, who satisfies his unconscious needs by introducing fiction into the factual record of his life – the invention of Clara and Baxter Dawes, for instance, Weiss argues, was predetermined by Lawrence's unconscious Oedipal drive. However, unlike Kuttner, Daniel Weiss does attend to the novel as art; to such matters as narrative point of view, patterns of imagery, scenes that derive from fairy tale, and the mythological pattern. He also draws several illuminating parallels with that other great Oedipal work, *Hamlet*. But he weakens his case at crucial points by pushing his interpretation too far, as for instance when he describes the burnt loaf becoming 'like the giant's egg in the fairy tale . . . the external repository of Gertrude's heart' [p.42]; or his argument that Mrs Morel's repressed fantasy drives her to push William's girls at his father, so as to leave William free for herself. The fundamental limitation of Daniel Weiss's analysis, however, is that there seems to be no boundary between the psychoanalytical and the realistic; what for Lawrence and his readers may be simply factual realism, in Weiss's interpretation is always pregnant with unconscious meaning.

A more general essay within the psychoanalytical school is Frank O'Connor's discussion of *Sons and Lovers* [1955], which brings in the neglected dimension of history. O'Connor argues that Paul idealises his mother for reasons that have to do with his being one of the newly educated working class created by the Education Act of 1870; because he aspires to the life of culture and purpose that his mother and Miriam both possess abundantly. However, for O'Connor too the Oedipus complex has its place in the making of the novel, though he interprets it rather differently from previous critics. In O'Connor's view, *Sons and Lovers* reveals Lawrence's psychological collapse and represents primarily a case-study in repressed homosexuality. Referring to John Middleton Murry's remark that Lawrence was attracted to Frieda's husband almost as much as he was to Frieda, O'Connor identifies Lawrence, and therefore Paul, as homosexual. Finding Paul's relationship with Clara Dawes unconvincing, he argues that Paul is really in love with Baxter and that consequently his rejection of Miriam represents the rejection of femininity within himself. Moreover, linking Lawrence with other major writers dominated by their mothers, who also wrote semi-autobiographical novels – Proust, Gide and Joyce – like Alfred Kuttner, Frank O'Connor sees this sexual deviance as symptomatic of profound changes in the cultural ethos of the period. Although its stress on homosexuality is crudely overemphatic, what is valuable in this eclectic but stimulating essay is O'Connor's attempt to build a bridge between psychoanalytical criticism and criticism which seeks to take account of the social and historical situation out of which the novel was written.

Psychoanalytical criticism found rich material to work with in *Sons and Lovers*, a novel which clearly has many points of affinity with Freud's Oedipus complex and which offers a penetrating study of psychological development. And on the whole such criticism offers valuable opportunities for gaining a deeper understanding of the novel's meaning, and of the nature of Lawrence's creative imagination. However, psychoanalytical criticism should be approached with circumspection, for even the subtler critics run the risk of forcing the text to serve a scientific theory; and in doing so they make three major assumptions: that there is a straightforward correspondence between Lawrence's own life and that of his fictional hero; that the author is a more or less passive medium for psychological discoveries, with little conscious control over the artistic shape and meaning of his fiction; and that the Oedipal relations in the novel exist divorced from the contexts of society and history.

Historical criticism

From its earliest reception critics have praised the authentic and powerful evocation of a historical community in *Sons and Lovers*. The first novel in English literature to treat working-class life in detail from the inside, it captures the atmosphere and rhythm of ordinary living in the Midlands coalfield at a crucial point in its development, when the older values of rural community life were being disrupted by industrialisation. Indeed, Lawrence himself was in the habit of referring to it as his 'colliery' novel. However, there was a tendency in early Lawrence criticism to neglect rather the historical dimension of *Sons and Lovers*. Critics concerned with the biographical sources of the novel, or with psychoanalysis, or with the form of fiction, relied on the text as a more or less straightforward representation of Lawrence's early life. Because they wished to illuminate the writer, his psychology, creative methods and imaginative vision, Bestwood was treated as the fictional extension of Lawrence's own mining community of Eastwood – as essentially background for the more important discussion of Lawrence's life, psyche and art. However, more recently, following the lead given by the Marxist historical critic Georg Lukács, English critics of Lawrence, notably Raymond Williams, have drawn attention to the importance of historical forces at work in his novels. This school of historical criticism is typically represented in recent Lawrence studies by the critical analyses of Scott Sanders [1973] and Graham Holderness [1982].

Scott Sanders begins his study of *Sons and Lovers* by acknowledging its autobiographical nature as a novel in which Lawrence sought to account for his own development from miner's son to artist, but he goes on to argue that, because this process cut Lawrence off from his father's people, he was unable to write objectively about the experience of growing-up in a working-class pit village:

> No one rivals Lawrence in the vividness with which he evokes the atmosphere of that industrial village, or the warring atmosphere of the home. But when it comes to passing judgement on that life, particularly upon Walter Morel, who is the only member of the family truly integrated into the mining community, Lawrence systematically distorts the picture [p.23].

For Scott Sanders this distortion has its roots in what he terms the 'formation' of Paul Morel, whose ideology of individualism, which he has absorbed from his mother, is close to that of Lawrence himself. During the first half of the novel Paul is engaged in learning his mother's middle-class values and language, which effectively exclude from their charmed circle not just his father but the whole Bestwood community. As Paul outstrips his mother's language, learning and ideas, Sanders argues, he turns first to Miriam, who is finally not articulate enough to satisfy him; and then as his social and aesthetic horizons expand he develops a sensibility alien to the Bestwood ethos. And his despair at the end of the novel is in large measure the despair of the *declassé* artist, who has fought free of his claustrophobic social background, but not in order to enter any fresh class or community. In Scott Sanders's view, because of his own individualist ideology, Lawrence refuses to regard social class as an issue in *Sons and Lovers*. Although Mrs Morel, a well-educated and idealistic Congregationalist, comes from the bourgeoisie, while her husband, a barely literate miner, prefers the public house to the chapel, Lawrence fails to recognise that the wreck of the Morels' marriage is caused by social differences. Paul Morel always sees the clash between his parents in psychological, or moral, terms and judges his father always from his mother's bourgeois perspective. However, in spite of the fact that for Lawrence the central problems in the novel are those of personal relationships, features of contemporary society do force themselves into *Sons and Lovers* in such a way that Lawrence presents, says Sanders, a 'fuller view of reality than his ideology would seem to allow for' [p.32], for his social realism undercuts the novel's dominant individualistic perspective, and this process, according to Engels and Lukács, is 'the triumph of realism' [p.32]. Thus, because Lawrence's moral judgements of the characters are often at odds with his social depiction of them, Paul is permitted by Lawrence to blame his father bitterly for being no more than a fairly typical representative of a social system, which the novel demonstrates is thwarting his life.

Lawrence's suppression of the connections implicit in the structure of the society of the novel Scott Sanders finds extending to his treatment of the four women whose lives impinge on Paul's – Mrs Morel, Miriam, Mrs Leivers and Clara. He fails to see their frustration and discontent, their intelligence and energy – which prompt them to seek outlets through their sons, their religion, their self-education and their feminism – in the historical context of the feminist movement of the period. Sanders's essential case against Lawrence in *Sons and Lovers* can be summarised as historical blindness. For all his detailed evocation of the conflicts of value within the pit community and his sense of its relation to the larger world beyond, because Lawrence's formation was fostered by the individualism of his mother, his focus is always on the psychological and the moral rather than the historical, and in *Sons and Lovers*, unlike his next novel, *The Rainbow*, Sanders concludes, Lawrence was 'largely unconscious of the impact of society on the individual' [p. 59].

This misconception is the result of Sanders's method of driving a wedge between what he regards as Paul's (and therefore Lawrence's) bourgeois individualist ideology, which he feels dominates the novel, and Lawrence's realistic depiction of the capitalist, industrial class society within which Paul lives. Moreover, Sanders's approach simplifies both the novel's ideology and its fictional values. His ideological argument would have been weakened by a formalist approach, for he does not take into account the way that those class concerns, which are rendered dramatically in the scenes of conflict between Mr and Mrs Morel, make an impact on the reader quite as powerful as Paul's individual moral judgements, delivered from his narrative point of view. And, when Sanders says that there 'seems to be a division between the narrator who is compassionately recording the miner's life, and the narrator who is judging that life' [p. 36], he is not only privileging the narrative point of view above the novel's other formal procedures, but arguing essentially that Lawrence has lost artistic control of his material. One of the reasons for this misapprehension is that Scott Sanders, like earlier critics, makes a rather too straightforward correlation between autobiography and fiction, between Lawrence and Paul Morel, which permits him to accept Paul's apparent ideology as the author's own. Sanders's case would also be weakened by the admission, which he rigorously excludes as a possibility, that Paul's formation possesses a psychological as well as a historical constituent – that it involves Freud as well as class – and so this major dimension of *Sons and Lovers* is virtually ignored.

Graham Holderness's historical approach is more thoroughly grounded in theory. As he says in his opening paragraph, the basis of his study is a materialist and historical theory of literature, which must presuppose 'that *all* literary productions . . . can be understood completely only by relating them to a historical and ideological context' [p.1]. In the case of *Sons and Lovers*, written by the son of a miner who was immersed in some of the most important historical movements of his period, the novel clearly contains history as its overt subject. However, Holderness challenges Lawrence's image of Eastwood as a semi-rural village and he takes issue with the formalist critics, who stress the author's own understanding of his society – seeing the detailed descriptions of Bestwood as either simple transcriptions from life, or as significant only because they represent Lawrence's imaginative vision. Although the structure of a novel is an analogy of the society it represents, Holderness contends that the historical critic must also take account of the Marxist view of ideology – that the writer's own relation to history is actually ideological. And, because the author is not a photographer, but an interpreter with his own political beliefs, the text of the novel also reproduces his ideology. From this point of view, like Scott Sanders, Graham Holderness sees the pressures within the society of Eastwood compelling Lawrence as a young writer to become increasingly isolated and individualist, while feeling at the same time the strong collective pull of communal experience. And this is embodied in *Sons and Lovers* in the experience of Paul Morel. Following Sanders, Holderness thus regards the Oedipus complex as an inadequate explanation for Paul's development, which for him has its roots in social conflict, and in particular the class conflict between his parents. Mrs Morel, who is acutely aware of herself as an individual apart from the community, is a major contributor to Paul's formation. Moreover, she represents one of the terms of his choice, while his father – who is integrated into the community and stands for its fellowship and values – represents the other.

Mrs Morel expresses most fully the individualist ideology of 'self-help', for although like the other women in the Women's Guild her membership is the register of her social aspiration, she possesses too a burning personal ambition to transcend the community by making her sons middle class; but, as William's career proves, this desire is destructive and futile. Although, says Holderness, Lawrence is never detached enough to criticise this ideology of self-help, he does dramatise a 'critique of the ideology by creating a social world in which, once the working-class community is left behind, there is precisely nothing "there"; there is in reality nowhere to go . . . Outside the working-class community there is nothing – a vacuum' [p.147].

Thus in Graham Holderness's view the concept of individuality must be understood both as a personal experience and as an ideology, in terms of the social pressures that formed it. Clearly Paul's individuality is also bound up with his desire to become an artist, which encourages him to develop in an even more individualistic way. However, because he is growing up in a culturally and emotionally rich community, he finally defeats these impulses which seek to transcend it. And Miriam and Clara are an important part of this process. Miriam teaches him to see reality as an internal essence within living things, but his deeper artistic instinct, developed by his strong links with the community and fostered by Clara, is for a more complete sense of wholeness, which includes Bestwood. Paul's unsuccessful sexual relationships are finally no substitute for the succour afforded by a community, to which he returns after his mother's death with an overwhelming sense of isolation. So, although Holderness describes the same process of progressive alienation as does Sanders, he differs in regarding the ties of community as being too strong to permit Paul to break them, in seeing this reinforced by his artistic instinct, and in regarding the conclusion of the novel as essentially optimistic.

Graham Holderness's emphasis on the social rather than the individual experience as a source of values is essentially limiting, and leads him to ignore the psychological dimension of personal conflict, for instance between Mr and Mrs Morel, even when, as in the scene of the cutting of William's hair, this is very much in evidence. Another area of weakness in his historical approach is his argument that the absence of the bourgeoisie is a 'significant absence', demonstrating that outside his community there is nowhere for a member of the working class to go. If, as the historical argument implies, Paul's ideological formation embodies the author's, then the conclusion of the novel should in theory mirror Lawrence's own resolution of this conflict. For Scott Sanders it does and Paul remains the *declassé* artist fearing social reabsorption, but for Graham Holderness Paul's artistic instinct leads him along a route that the historical Lawrence did not take.

However, Scott Sanders's and Graham Holderness's historical analyses of *Sons and Lovers* are stimulating and properly draw the reader's attention to a neglected area of the novel – to Lawrence's acute sense of social values, his awareness of the significance of social pressures, his feeling for human solidarity, and his evocation of the experience of growing up in a particular, concretely realised historical society. But their attempt to apply to *Sons and Lovers* a fairly complex theory, and to evaluate the novel from an ideological perspective, leads to some narrow and rather dogmatic assumptions, especially in their discussion of the relative values of individualism and collectivism. Moreover, the historical critics leave much of the novel in shadow; its Oedipal dimension, so overwhelmingly important for the early Freudian critics, is neglected. Also a good deal of the novel's meaning is simplified by regarding the main characters – Walter and Gertrude Morel, Miriam and Clara, and also Baxter Dawes – as valuable for their typical and representative quality rather than for their psychological or moral uniqueness. This is indicative of the tendency of historical criticism to look at the novel as evidence rather than as art, minimising the complexity of the narrative by insisting, as Sanders does, on the dominance of Paul's uncorrected point of view throughout the novel, or, as Holderness does, on the centrality of the scenes of class conflict; while both of them deal with the central section of the novel, Paul's relationship with Miriam, which does not readily lend itself to historical interpretation, in a perfunctory way. The limitations of historical criticism in treating a novel as rich and complex as *Sons and Lovers* can be seen in the fact that Scott Sanders and Graham Holderness disagree on the fundamental point of the extent to which Lawrence was aware of the influence of society on people's individuality. Sanders's view is that, because Lawrence was virtually oblivious to the impact of society on the individual, realism triumphs unconsciously in *Sons and Lovers*; while Holderness believes that Lawrence's autobiographical realist method insists that individuality 'must always be understood in the context of the social forces and pressures which produce it, as an experience and as an ideology' [p. 149]. The fact that two sensitive historical critics can arrive at such different conclusions about both the novel's ending and Lawrence's understanding of the relation between the individual and society indicates how resistant great art is to the schematising effect of ideological criticism, and suggests that historical criticism as yet lacks an adequate aesthetic.

Feminist criticism

Beginning perhaps with Virginia Woolf's revolutionary plea for social justice for women in *A Room of One's Own* [1928] and stimulated by Simone de Beauvoir's classic polemic *The Second Sex* [1949], there has developed, especially in the years following the publication of Kate Millett's *Sexual Politics* [1970], an identifiable political school of feminist criticism. However, as Terry Eagleton has put it, the feminist critic is 'not studying representations of gender simply because she believes that this will further her political ends. She also believes that gender and sexuality are central themes in literature and other sorts of discourse, and that any critical account which suppresses them is seriously defective' [1983, p. 209]. Naturally Lawrence's novels have been a major focus of feminist interest. He has been praised for his intuitive understanding and sensitive portrayal of women by critics as different in period and style as Anaïs Nin [1932] and Lydia Blanchard [1975], who have vigorously defended Lawrence's sympathy for the social plight of intelligent women trapped in a male-dominated society. However, feminist criticism on the whole has been severe on Lawrence. John Middleton Murry, in *Son of Woman*, published in 1931 [*Casebook*, pp. 95–105], was the first to accuse Lawrence of wishing in his fiction to annihilate the female and rehabilitate the male; but Simone de Beauvoir was the first feminist critic to attempt to politicise the reader's response to what she regarded as Lawrence's faith in male supremacy, his feeling that a woman's role is primarily sexual, and his fear of the modern woman's raised consciousness. And in *Sons and Lovers* she sees Paul expecting first Miriam and then Clara to give up personal, individualised love for an impersonal force in which the female worships the male.

This argument is part of Simone de Beauvoir's much larger polemic, but it forms the basis for a later, more thorough-going attack on Lawrence from Kate Millett. However, although Millett is scathing about Lawrence's treatment of women in *The Rainbow* and *Women in Love*, she has some difficulty in sustaining her argument when she considers *Sons and Lovers*. On the one hand she suggests that Paul Morel is upheld by a 'faith in male supremacy which he has imbibed from his father and enlarged upon himself' [p.249]. Yet on the other hand this ideological critique conflicts with her more generous judgement of the novel's art. For her, *Sons and Lovers* is a great novel because it embodies profoundly felt experience and is 'probably still the greatest novel of proletarian life in English' [p. 247]. The weakness of Millett's approach is that her ideological view of *Sons and Lovers* is allowed to override her aesthetic response to it as art.

Characteristic of much feminist criticism – as seen earlier with historical criticism – is the equation of fiction with life, which denies Paul the objective status of a fictional, picaresque hero figure, whose adventures and development we follow. Millett also denies the novel the interest of a psychological study, for to acknowledge it would seriously weaken her polemic. For instance, she affirms that Paul's Oedipal fixation is 'rather less a matter of the son's passion for the mother than his passion for attaining the level of power to which adult male status is supposed to entitle him' [pp. 247–8]. For her Paul represents the male ego rampant, and the novel's women exist to serve him: Miriam in the role of disciple, Clara to remove his sexual inhibitions, and Mrs Morel to motivate his artistic and social ambitions. Moreover, Millett argues, there is an element of sadism in Paul's treatment of Miriam and Clara, who are finally dispensed with, together with his mother, 'so that he may venture forth and inherit the great masculine world which awaits him' [p. 252]. However, this critical judgement ignores all those factors – psychological, familial, social and historical – that make up Paul's identity and situation. Equally, it does not take account of the bleak tone of the novel's concluding section.

Moreover, Kate Millett's determination to read the novel as a case-study of male egotism leads her to misread its structure, which she regards as not only dominated by Paul's point of view, but also as broken-backed: 'While the first half of *Sons and Lovers* is perfectly realised, the second part is deeply flawed by Lawrence's overparticipation in Paul's endless scheming to disentangle himself from the persons who have helped him most' [p. 254]. This interpretation derives from a feminist posture which identifies too closely with both Miriam and Clara. For instance, Millett reads sexual politics into such incidents as the occasion when Paul throws a pencil in Miriam's face during an algebra lesson, which Millett interprets in Freudian terms as an assault with his penis, when in fact at that point in the novel Lawrence seems to be exploring the cultural rather than the sexual gulf between Paul and Miriam. Similarly, she identifies strongly with Clara, who, she argues, is brought by Paul to regard her feminism as merely a substitute for a satisfying sexual relationship, whereas in truth Clara's taking back her submissive husband is her supreme assertion of independence. While Kate Millett's approach to *Sons and Lovers* is valuable because of its fresh attention to matters of gender and sexuality and its lively polemic (and in spite of her intuitive critical sympathy with the novel), her endeavour to politicise the reader's response in accordance with her feminist ideology produces a patchy and sometimes quirky interpretation. She confuses fiction with life, ignores the relations between the individual characters and their historical community, denies the Freudian level of the novel any really significant status, identifies too closely with the women characters, and essentially regards the novel as a broken-backed vehicle of sexual fascism.

Kate Millett's influence as a feminist critic is evident in Faith Pullin's essay on *Sons and Lovers* [1978]. She too regards Lawrence as a 'ruthless user of women . . . the mother, Miriam and Clara are all manipulated in Paul's painful effort at self-identification' [p. 49]. Her main purpose is to demonstrate how Lawrence employs his women characters to study the male psyche, and in doing so, like Millett, she permits her ideological strategy to blur the distinction betweeen fiction and autobiography. Because she identifies with both the betrayed Jessie Chambers and the rejected Miriam Leivers, she refers to Jessie's bitterness at having been cast in the novel as a disciple rather than as an intellectual equal, without acknowledging Lawrence's creative transformation of life into art – of historical relationships into fictional ones. Pullin follows Millett, too, in seeing a brutal insensitivity in Paul's treatment of Miriam, but also in his sense of titillation at being Clara's boss as well as her lover.

Like Kate Millett, Faith Pullin plays down the role of cultural determinants implicit in the working-class patriarchy within which Paul lives, in order to lay bare Lawrence's own psychic conflicts; and once again the Freudian pattern in Paul's relationships is suppressed in favour of an ideological reading of what she identifies as the sub-text of *Sons and Lovers*, which she regards as 'condemning Mrs Morel for her stifling hold on Paul', and which reveals that 'the true love in Sons and Lovers is between Paul and his father. His deepest adolescent desire is to be a painter, a creator and celebrator of life, like his father' [p. 52]. This pursuit of the novel's sub-text leads Pullin into several erroneous judgements, omissions and suppressions. She leans too heavily on Lawrence's own faulty description of the novel in his letter to Garnett, which she elaborates by asserting that William was the lover of whom Paul was jealous; while the closeness of her focus on Paul's relationship with Miriam as being the core of the novel leaves several of its relationships and areas of narrative interest out of consideration, especially when she claims that the Clara episode is redundant. She also regards the novel as inartistic and untruthful because it is highly schematic, and therefore for her the richly conceived characters of Mrs Morel, Miriam and Clara are only stereotypes, because the author 'fell into the trap of producing diagrams, rather than portraits. Lawrence's psychic history meant that, in spite of his often brilliant insights, he was unable to represent women as they are' [p. 73]. Although Faith Pullin's approach offers some useful comment on the complexity of Paul's relationship with his father, her polemical criticism is not primarily concerned with the realistic portrayal of lives in a historical community, nor with the development of a profound psychological drama, but with a narrowly political assessment of Lawrence's sexual ideology. Her final judgement of the value of Sons and Lovers – that it reveals Lawrence's failure to depict women truthfully – is the result of a reductive ideological method of critical analysis, and is a further example of feminist criticism finding itself unable to bridge the gulf between a political critique and literary criticism.

Hilary Simpson [1982] offers a corrective to Faith Pullin's relegation of the Clara Dawes section of the novel, for she concentrates much of her attention on Clara as a feminist and also on the feminist consciousness of Mrs Morel. Simpson is concerned to suggest a new basis for the discussion of Lawrence's writing, by examining his treatment of sexual relationships and roles 'in relation to selected aspects of women's history and the development of feminism' [p. 15]. In Sons and Lovers she is particularly interested in Lawrence's response to the women's suffrage movement, for, as she demonstrates, in his early life Lawrence was surrounded by women who were involved in the campaign. Like Mrs Morel, Lawrence's mother was an official of the local Co-operative Women's Guild, and he was himself a close friend of progressive socialists, like the Hopkins and the Daxes in Eastwood. Jessie Chambers's brother remembered 'rampageous arguments on politics, especially votes for women, with Lawrence leading the younger generation against their parents' [p. 21]; while Louie Burrows, to whom Lawrence was engaged for a time, was deeply involved in the suffrage campaign.

It is clear that for a brief period in his early development as a novelist Lawrence took up the cause of feminism, feeling that his novels would do more for women than the suffrage, as he wrote to a friend from Eastwood. It is also plain that, while he accepted the traditional definitions of masculinity and femininity, he supported the concept of equality between the sexes. Lawrence's feminism emerges early in *Sons and Lovers*, first in his sympathetic analysis of the situation of Mrs Morel and later in that of Clara Dawes, both of which reveal the oppression of a patriarchal society that inspired the women's movement. Lawrence clearly understands the value of the reciprocal impact of Mrs Morel's membership of the Women's Guild on herself and her children, and also the resentment of the miners, who find this new view of their wives disconcerting; but he is grimly aware that the Guild cannot change the essential conditions of Mrs Morel's life.

Because the situation of Clara Dawes, who was partly based on Alice Dax, is so different from that of Mrs Morel, Hilary Simpson argues, it seems that her feminism will loom large in the story. An active feminist for ten years, Clara intrigues Paul, but eventually the novel implies that Clara's dissatisfaction has to do with her own sexuality and, agreeing with Kate Millett, Simpson concludes that 'the character of Clara lacks coherence; her feminism, one of the major characteristics through which she is first defined for us, ultimately has no real function' [p. 29]. This is because Paul overcomes her feminist independence with old-fashioned chivalry and encourages her to believe that what she really needs is sexual fulfilment. He sees feminist issues as personal issues rather than general ones. His response to her comment about women's sweated work, when she is lace-making, is to get her back her job at Jordan's. And, when Paul advocates sexual freedom, he ignores her position in a society which demands that a woman's main means of self-definition must be through love and marriage. However, unlike Millett, Simpson finds Clara's return to her husband quite convincing, for she never quite cut him adrift, and it also represents an aspect of her feminist independence. While Paul wants submission from Clara, Baxter Dawes is emotionally dependent on his wife and offers her a relationship which she can dominate.

Hilary Simpson's account of the novel, although deliberately limited in focus, is valuable for the way it gives a historical context to Lawrence's sense of sexual politics. Her documentation of women's history offers evidence for a revised literary analysis of this aspect of the novel. She concludes that the 'real blow to feminism in *Sons and Lovers* lies in Lawrence's failure to connect the personal world of individual development to the larger material forces which have a part in shaping it. Because it has no anchor in the material world, Clara's feminism comes to seem merely an extraneous detail, as though Lawrence had given her a squint' [p. 37]. But more generally she demonstrates how in this novel Lawrence responded to the feminism of his own day, and her tactful forging of connections between history and fiction is fruitful in revealing Lawrence's generosity of spirit.

Feminist criticism ranges from an appreciation of Lawrence's understanding of women and of their social and historical situation to a somewhat shrill condemnation of his alleged male chauvinism. Critics such as Kate Millett juxtapose a positive critical response to the novel's art with an ideological attack on its treatment of women; while others, such as Hilary Simpson, combine scholarship with judicious criticism, in order to demonstrate Lawrence's feminist sympathies, and to pin-point at the same time precisely where she believes his feminist theme falls away under the stress of his interest in Paul Morel. In general feminist criticism has been valuable in opening up *Sons and Lovers* to political interpretation. Gender and sexuality are obviously central issues in the novel and it is important to understand Lawrence's attitude towards them. However, characteristic limitations of feminist criticism include a failure to distinguish adequately

between autobiography and fiction – a too simple equation of
Paul Morel with Lawrence himself – and a marked tendency to
identify with the women characters, which produces a narrow
focus and leads to distortions of judgement. Moreover, the
ideological nature of feminist criticism minimises the
importance of those cultural and Oedipal determinants which
make up Paul's complex situation. But, most importantly,
feminist criticism does not seem to have developed the capacity
to offer a committed political perspective, while at the same
time giving proper critical attention to the aesthetic properties
and artistic complexity of Lawrence's fiction, feeling perhaps
that to do so might dilute the force of its polemic. Yet not to do
so weakens the authority of its criticism.

Formalist criticism

By 'formalist criticism' I mean a broad critical approach which
seeks to understand a work of fiction by attending to the way the
author's imaginative vision inheres in the novel in a significant
form. However, the precise meaning of the term 'form' depends
upon the particular critic's focus of interest. The influential
formalist school of New Criticism, for instance, isolates the text
for examination, separating it both from its author's intentions
and from the reader's response. The text is abstracted from its
social and historical contexts, and is regarded as a distinct
artefact, which possesses its own inner coherence and complex
organic unity. And clearly the genre most appropriate as the
subject of this methodology is poetry.

Dorothy Van Ghent [1953] therefore approaches *Sons and
Lovers* as essentially a poetic novel. She is concerned to argue
that the novel is constructed around an idea that finds its finest
articulation in the poetic structure, which she distinguishes
from the realistic chronological plan. For her Lawrence seeks to
show how possessiveness in human relations is a destructive
force, and this 'controlling idea is expressed in the various
episodes – the narrative logic of the book. It is also expressed in
imagery – the book's poetic logic. Perhaps in no other novelist
do we find the image so largely replacing episode and discursive
analysis, and taking over the expressive functions of these, as it
does in Lawrence' [*Casebook*, p. 114]. Through the medium of
symbolism, Lawrence makes us aware of the rhythms of the life

force which the natural creature obeys – the plants symbolising its phallic power, when Mrs Morel is locked out in the moonlit garden; the sacred individuality of the wren's nest that Paul discovers; the red stallion, which represents the impersonal sexual power that will drive Paul from Miriam to Clara; the pecking of the hen when Miriam offers it maize, which embodies the mysterious energy working through Paul and Miriam; or the more obvious symbolism of the spilling of the red carnations on Clara's clothes and on the ground, when she and Paul first make love beside the Trent.

According to Dorothy Van Ghent, only in one character in *Sons and Lovers*, Walter Morel, 'does the biological life force have simple, unequivocal assertion' [*Casebook*, p. 120]. His possession of this creative energy is manifested in that masculine integrity his wife and children find so attractive on those special occasions, which operate as realistic symbols – taking his bath, or making fuses – when he is part of the family. And his daily descent into the black depths of the coal mine, Van Ghent regards as a complex, ambivalent symbol of sexuality and nature, which, although rooted in grim historical reality, is nevertheless symbolic of 'the greater rhythm governing life and obedience to which is salvation' [*Casebook*, p. 120]. The denial of this fundamental vitalism, the corruption of selfhood through the craving for possession, is also rendered symbolically, argues Van Ghent – for instance in Miriam's attitude towards the flowers, or in Clara's determination to resist the reality of Paul's individuality in that scene of their love-making, in spite of their awed awareness of the life force flowing through them, symbolised by the cry of the peewits and the wheel of the stars. Van Ghent comments that Clara's is the 'impulse toward personal possessorship that constantly confuses and distorts human relationships in Lawrence's books; it is a denial of the otherness of people, and a denial, really, of the great inhuman life force, the primal "otherness" through which people have their independent definition as well as their creative community' [*Casebook*, p. 127]. It is this force that Paul was in touch with when in the garden at night he responded to the coarse scent of the iris and made his decision to break with Miriam, and which sustains him in his relationship with Clara.

Dorothy Van Ghent quotes with approval the judgement of

André Malraux and Stephen Spender that Lawrence is concerned only with the nature of being and with the non-human; and she adds that this can be understood 'only in the context of twentieth century man's resignation to herd ideologies, herd recreations, herd rationalisations' [*Casebook*, p. 127]. Politically of course Van Ghent's approach is at the opposite pole to historical criticism, which espouses the view that people can only realise their full humanity within a community; while, in its retreat from this ideology, New Critical formalism stresses a form of individualism which is sometimes concerned with human existence as an expression of the life force. However, Van Ghent's discussion is important for its emphasis on the function of non-human nature in human experience, for its defence of Walter Morel, and for its insistence on the presence of a level of poetic, symbolic meaning in the novel. However, the strength and coherence of her argument is counterbalanced by the limitations of her method. She privileges a spatial account of the novel over the dominant chronological record of experience, for her interest does not lie in those areas which depend on the chronological narrative – the Freudian view of Paul's development, or the view of *Sons and Lovers* as a novel of education of the hero into a particular historical society; and theoretically in her analysis the pattern of imagery can be read in any order. This choice of critical strategy also marginalises the extent to which *Sons and Lovers* draws on other formal conventions: for instance, in those scenes of domestic conflict around which some historical critics argue the novel is organised, and which depend for their success on Lawrence's dramatic sense. Moreover, her approach ignores the conventional view of character as being interesting to the reader for reasons of psychology, morality or class attitudes. For her characters are only important in so far as they respond to the life force, so that, while Paul Morel, the hero, is dealt with briefly, Walter Morel is allocated a disproportionate amount of discussion. It follows that, except for the strained reference to the symbolism of the coal mine, the social and historical perspectives of the novel are entirely absent from her analysis. Dorothy Van Ghent's critical method stresses the novel's status as a self-enclosed value system – lifted for the purpose of analysis out of its network of autobiographical and historical connections – which possesses a unity given by what she calls its 'poetic logic'. In effect the narrative framework exists as a peg on which to hang the thematic and symbolic pattern, and this sense of closure and completion works against our sense of the novel's realism.

In another narrowly focused essay, Seymour Betsky [1953] argues for a thematic and formalist interpretation of *Sons and Lovers* based, not on its poetic logic, but on what he discerns as its rhythmic structure. For him the novel's pattern is determined by the quality of its human relationships, which display a wave-like rhythm as they build to a consummation and then diminish in intensity. For instance, Paul's relationship with his mother reaches its peak after his brother William's death, and then begins to decline when he leaves home, although he returns compulsively to that relationship again and again. Similarly, the marriage of Walter and Gertrude Morel had achieved its consummation before the main action of the novel begins, and we observe the gradual slackening of its emotional power. In Betsky's view, Lawrence's description of *Sons and Lovers* in his letter to Garnett directs the reader to read the novel thematically, as the story of Lawrence's attempt to purge himself of his past experience – a view shared by F.R. Leavis [1955. pp. 19–20]. Thus for Betsky the most successful areas of the novel, because they involve Lawrence's catharsis, are those which focus on Mrs Morel, which are fully realised by Paul's wave-like relation to his mother; while Paul's relationship with Miriam loses this distinctive pulse and the 'defeat of Miriam fritters to a most unconvincing series of "perhapses", fatally for the "Miriam" portion of the novel' [*Casebook*, p. 139].

This essay is useful principally for the way it throws into relief an important dimension of Lawrence's artistic creation of relationships by means of a fictional pattern – rhythm. Betsky's argument becomes blurred, however, when he identifies this rhythm too closely with what he defines as the dominant Freudian theme, for the crucial relationship between Paul's parents is not shown to be connected with this theme; while the rhythm of Paul's relationship with Clara is not explored at all. Although Seymour Betsky detects the presence of the later Lawrence of *The Rainbow* and *Women in Love* in his 'rhythmic control of theme, intelligence controlling the blood-beat' [*Casebook*, p. 139], and in his use of symbolism, *Sons and Lovers*, he argues, fails to achieve the status of a major novel because its artist theme is subordinated to its Freudian theme, and because Lawrence does not engage in the exploration of the plight of his civilisation. However, this limited view derives from Betsky's close thematic focus and from his wish to look at the novel retrospectively in the context of Lawrence's later work.

In order to embody his ideas formally in his fiction, the novelist employs technique, which Mark Schorer [1948] regards as the writer's only means of exploring, conveying and evaluating his subject. For Schorer technique is also a means of achieving objectivity; but in *Sons and Lovers*, he argues, because Lawrence is impatient with technique he loses this objectivity and confuses the novel's meanings. The two themes of the novel – Mrs Morel's emotional crippling of her son, and the 'split' between Paul's physical and spiritual love – do not work together as they should, and Paul's 'drift towards death', as his letter to Garnett describes it, is reversed by the novel's optimistic ending. This gulf, Schorer continues, reveals a contradiction, particularly in the case of Walter and Gertrude Morel, between Lawrence's creation and evaluation of character, which derives technically from Lawrence's sharing Paul's point of view. Paul and Lawrence both have a love–hate relationship with each of the parents, which constitutes for Schorer a 'psychological tension which disrupts the form of the novel and obscures its meaning, because neither the contradiction in style nor the confusion in point of view is made to right itself. Lawrence is merely repeating his emotions, and he avoids an austerer technical scrutiny of his material because it would compel him to master them' [*Casebook*, pp. 109–10].

Mark Schorer is taken to task by Barbara Hardy [1964] over his New Critical notions of form and truth, because he presupposes an inappropriate concept of form based on a circumscribed view of clarity, unity and conclusiveness. As she points out, Lawrence is vulnerable to the kind of formal approach employed by Schorer precisely because he resists the schematic, refusing the temptation to offer stereotypical characters – the hateful father, the sympathetic mother, and Paul as the passive victim of her claustrophobic love. Schorer's preference for Jessie Chambers's account of Lawrence's failure in love is prompted, Hardy suggests, by the appeal of the 'classical schematism of an Oedipal pattern and the classical schematism of unity and simplicity. Both seem to be at the back of Schorer's key comment: 'The point of view is never adequately objectified and sustained to tell us which is true.' Truth had no simple or single face for Lawrence' [p. 140]. Lawrence saw that human relations are mixed and complex, so that Paul's weakness for his mother's love is not 'disguised', as Schorer suggests, by Miriam's insistence on spiritual love. Indeed, if Lawrence had wished to make Miriam the scapegoat, as Hardy points out, he would have treated Clara Dawes very differently, or omitted her altogether. Finally, Hardy challenges Schorer's assertion that the final paragraph of the novel is not the logical conclusion to the 'crippling effects of a mother's love' [*Casebook*, p. 110], by drawing attention to the fact that 'crippling' is not Lawrence's word, that the mother's death is presented as a 'conscious product of knowing and wishing which will free Paul' [p. 145] and that there is a good deal of evidence in the novel that Paul will choose life. Barbara Hardy rightly regards Mark Schorer's diagnosis of the failure of Lawrence's technique in *Sons and Lovers* as flawed because it rests on too narrow a definition of form, behind which lies too limited an estimation of Lawrence's view of the complex truth of human growth and relationships. Schorer's emphasis on detachment and objectivity, clarity and unity, is baffled by Lawrence's realistic and truthful rendering of the complex and inherently contradictory nature of human experience.

Julian Moynahan [1963] interprets the term 'form' in a broader and more complex way than Mark Schorer, but more schematically than Barbara Hardy, arguing that *Sons and Lovers* has

> three formal orders or matrices, which inhabit the same serial order of narrated words. To a degree, they blend with each other, and enrich one another. The first matrix is autobiographical narrative; the second a scheme taken over from psychoanalytic theory; the third is difficult to name because Lawrence was the first novelist to use it as a context, as opposed to a quality, of human experience, but it might be called the matrix of 'life' [p. 14].

The autobiographical narrative articulates the novel's historical sequence of events; the psychoanalytic structure depends on the Freudian interpretation of behaviour; and the vital matrix is defined by the logic of life. Our sustained interest in Paul's growing-up makes him the hero of an autobiographical novel; in its psychological framework he is an example of Oedipal fixation; while in terms of vitalism he is a quester whose every choice is for or against life. And each of these three formal orders, suggests Moynahan, has its own appropriate mode of expression: the autobiographical element is conveyed by the naturalistic surface; the psychoanalytical level is implicit within the autobiographical, but is pointed up by the author's commentary; and the vitalistic level informs both naturalistic narrative and commentary, and is also expressed dramatically in intense scenes and in vivid poetic passages.

Having accomplished his primary aim of defending Lawrence against the charge of formlessness in *Sons and Lovers*, Julian Moynahan then employs his formal model to explain why several critics have nevertheless been right in feeling that there is formal confusion in the novel. It arises, says Moynahan, because of a conflict between the psychoanalytical and the vital contexts. As an Oedipal man, Paul is trapped in a neurosis from which only therapy can free him; yet, as a vital hero, Paul manages to preserve his identity and freedom and grow into an independent adult. However, for Moynahan, the ambiguous conclusion of the novel goes some way towards resolving this formal problem. Paul stands on the brink of disintegration, but still has his mysterious life and will. He has acted freely in separating himself from his mother, yet this freedom isolates him from the world. Although the ending is finely balanced, it is possible, says Moynahan, to regard Paul as setting out on a quest for wholeness and connection. In the novel's colliery world freedom is severely limited. However, for Lawrence, argues Moynahan, the individual 'is rooted in life as well as history and cannot escape his own freedom to make the choices that life will judge by an inscrutable morality', and he continues, 'Paul Morel is the proper hero of *Sons and Lovers* because he holds and uses this freedom in a greater measure than any other character. He imposes himself' [p.23].

In many ways Julian Moynahan's analysis is characteristic of the moralist influence on the formalist approach to Lawrence, established by F.R. Leavis [1955] and evident, for instance, in the critical strategy of Keith Sagar's later essay on *Sons and Lovers* [*Casebook*, pp. 208–15]. Moynahan's interpretation is persuasive and goes some way towards explaining previous critics' opinion that it was formless, or that at best it suffered from a confusion of aims that was reflected in a degree of muddle within its form. However, because he invokes a hierarchy of structural matrices, he views Paul's growing-up in society essentially as realistic narrative background. Moynahan's critical strategy reduces the novel to two alternative interpretations, the Freudian and the vitalistic, which represent a choice between determinism and freedom; and clearly for him what he defines as life finally succeeds in overcoming the deterministic pressures of the psychoanalytic pattern. However, Moynahan has difficulty in defining precisely quite what is meant by 'vitalism' – something at once less narrow and more moral than Dorothy Van Ghent's almost mystical concept. Yet there is something faintly disturbing about the intense individualism of his unreserved commendation of Paul's assertion of will over Miriam, Clara and finally his mother, which leads him to judge Mrs Morel's will to live in spite of her terminal cancer as destructive, simply because it is emotionally problematic for Paul, and to ignore the fact that she vainly wills herself to die. This tendency to adopt Paul's point of view uncritically goes hand in hand with Julian Moynahan's willingness to employ Lawrence's own terminology in his criticism. Both are in evidence when he endorses Paul's judgement of his father's unwillingness to look on his dead wife as a refusal of the 'life' within him. And Moynahan accepts without demure Lawrence's erroneous statement in his letter to Garnett that the tie of blood makes the mother dominant and that the Freudian 'split' leads to William's death. Equally important is Moynahan's tendency to diminish the historical context, which is relegated to background naturalism. But most important is the way his matrix theory stresses the separateness of experience, rather than suggesting – which is what we feel when we read the novel – that the Freudian, the vitalistic, the social and indeed the aesthetic (for Paul is also an artist) are all inextricably intertwined aspects of Paul's unique experience of growing-up.

Criticism which attends to the novel's formal dimension – its structural patterns – allows access to certain significant areas of the author's creative imagination as it is embodied within the text: in poetic symbolism, which transcends the linear narrative; in profounder emotional rhythms; and in the complex articulation of different levels of meaning. However,

apart from Barbara Hardy, these critics share a concern with
values that are generated by the text itself, divorced from
external influences, and so they take little account of the context
of village life and of Paul's representative historical function.
Moreover, they are strongly influenced by the aesthetic values
of classical simplicity and unity, which Dorothy Van Ghent
discovers in the novel's 'poetic logic'; which Seymour Betsky
discerns in its rhythm; and which is preserved in the
schematism of Julian Moynahan's ampler analysis. And this is
reinforced by their need to identify a thematic unity in *Sons and
Lovers*. Van Ghent detects a controlling idea; Betsky discovers a
strong Freudian theme which submerges a secondary theme of
Paul the artist; Schorer laments a division between two themes
(Paul's crippling by his mother, and his 'split' between physical
and spiritual love); and Moynahan offers an analysis of the
conflict between the Freudian theme and the dominant
vitalistic theme. This preoccupation with form in a limited
sense also extends to the novel's rhetoric, for, apart from
Schorer (who raises the subject only to disparage it), formalist
critics tend to ignore Lawrence's endeavours both to achieve
artistic detachment and also to influence the reader's response.
From a political point of view, this kind of criticism is highly
individualistic and lacking on the whole a qualifying
liberal-humanist perspective. By contrast, however, Barbara
Hardy eschews the narrow notion of form founded on thematic
unity, or on the Oedipal pattern, and her quarrel with Mark
Schorer embodies a more flexible, liberal view of the novel's
form, and one which takes account of Lawrence's endeavour to
tell the whole truth about highly complex human situations.

Genre criticism

As a novel concerned with the process of growing-up, *Sons and
Lovers* belongs to a genre known as the *Bildungsroman*. The most
sensitive study of the novel from this critical point of view is that
of Jerome Hamilton Buckley [1974] who notes that the
Bildungsroman has been defined as the '"novel of all-around
development or self-culture" with "a more or less conscious
attempt on the part of the hero to integrate his powers, to
cultivate himself by his experience"' [p. 13]. As Buckley points

out, in England the *Bildungsroman* has also often been a *Künstlerroman* – a story about the growth of an artist. Just as in James Joyce's *A Portrait of the Artist as a Young Man* Stephen Dedalus is learning to be a poet, or in Dickens's *David Copperfield* David is an apprentice prose-writer, so in *Sons and Lovers* Paul is an aspiring painter. Typically, this genre offers a study of the development of the inner world of the artist from childhood through adolescence to young manhood, and, as in the case of Joyce, or Lawrence, the study is frequently close to autobiography. Herein lies the strength and weakness of the *Bildungsroman*, for the novelist must both draw on the immediate and authentic in his experience, and at the same time transcend it in order to achieve objectivity and artistic integrity.

Focusing on English and European examples of the genre, Jerome Buckley reveals a common pattern of experience which *Sons and Lovers* shares and which he summarises thus: 'childhood, the conflict of generations, provinciality, the larger society, self-education, alienation, ordeal by love, the search for a vocation and a working philosophy' [p. 18]. In this pattern the growing child, if not actually fatherless, is repelled, like Stephen Dedalus and Paul Morel, by a father he mistrusts and who seeks to thwart his desires. And this is paralleled by his loss of faith in the values of home and family. The flight from home is also to some degree an escape from provinciality, but the city is an ambivalent symbol of promise, and, before his initiation into the adult world is complete, the hero is further tested by the ordeal of love. As Buckley points out, Paul's love affairs fall into a pattern common to other *Bildungsromane* – an experience of spiritual love and fleshly love, represented by Miriam and Clara – which are stages in the hero's conscious development. Paul also shares with other heroes, such as David Copperfield and Stephen Dedalus, an acute aesthetic sensibility. Both its early title, *Paul Morel*, and the way the novel follows a common pattern, Buckley argues, suggest Lawrence's conscious intention of focusing his narrative on a single hero figure and of adopting this particular form. For Lawrence was aware of the history of this genre before he began writing *Sons and Lovers*. Not only did he tell Jessie Chambers that he admired the way autobiography and fiction were inextricably mixed in George Borrow's *Lavengro*, but he also knew *Wilhelm Meister*, *The Red and the Black, David Copperfield,* and *Jude the Obscure,* works which Buckley suggests offered ways of adapting to the genre material which was highly personal. However, Jerome Buckley regards *Sons and Lovers* as structurally flawed by the pressure of personal experience. In the realistic first half of the novel Lawrence triumphantly presents his own past with objectivity and visual intensity, but the second half is dominated by Paul's personal problems and by analysis rather than description, so that the story 'takes on the aspect of a typical case history, such as the paradigmatic naming of a late chapter "Passion" or the change of title from the specific *Paul Morel* to the generalised *Sons and Lovers* might suggest' [p. 217]. Paul's mother fixation becomes increasingly insistent in the later chapters, which in Buckley's view invite a Freudian interpretation, for, like Alfred Kuttner, Jerome Buckley sees Paul as 'one of the many sick heroes of modern literature whose psychic wound is not soon healed' [p. 220]. In this argument, Paul's wayward temperament and Nietzschean individualism are condoned by Lawrence because Paul is an artist. However, Paul's artistic individuality cannot survive his mother's death, for he can no longer paint, and, although at the end he is marginally more inclined to life than to death, in hinting at his ultimate recovery, says Buckley, Lawrence is drawing on his own experience and being untrue to the logic of the story.

The main strengths of Jerome Buckley's critical approach are twofold. In drawing attention to Lawrence's awareness that he was writing *Sons and Lovers* within the conventions of a particular genre, he alerts us to the conscious, shaping process that is going on in the text; and he also reminds us of the degree of artistic objectivity and artistic integrity that Lawrence achieves in this novel. Further, Buckley does not strive to fit *Sons and Lovers* into a rigid *Bildungsroman* mould, but focuses with sensitivity on Lawrence's highly individual use of the genre. However, this approach also has its limitations. The close correspondence between the form of autobiography and that of the *Bildungsroman,* Buckley argues, makes the first half of the novel especially powerful, while the second half is a case history, resulting in the creation of a different kind of novel precisely at the point of Paul's emergence into adulthood. But this view fails to take account of the clear Freudian pattern developed in the early part of the novel, which works its way inexorably into the second part. Moreover, in his treatment of the novel's conclusion, Buckley's endeavour to prove his thesis that it is very difficult to integrate autobiographical material into the *Bildungsroman* with sufficient detachment prevents him from seeing the novel's conclusion as realistically ambivalent and appreciating Lawrence's success in keeping autobiographical material at a proper distance. Further, because Buckley focuses on the education of Paul Morel as the hero of a *Bildungsroman*, he tends to neglect the wider, complex function of society in his development from the narrow confines of a pit community to the ampler social spaces of the big city.

The contribution of *Sons and Lovers* to the *Künstlerroman* tradition is discussed by Maurice Beebe [1964], who speculates that but for the influence of Frieda's Freudianism the earlier versions of the novel might have been closer to that tradition, emphasising more strongly than the final text does the development of Paul Morel as an artist. Referring to Lawrence's letter to Garnett, Beebe argues, 'The obvious inadequacy of Lawrence's understanding of the book he had written lends support to the view that *Sons and Lovers* contains a buried theme that enabled Lawrence subconsciously to resolve conflicts which are unsolvable on the conscious level' [*Casebook*, p. 179]. Beebe's case essentially is that Lawrence's creative energy finally overcame the sterility of the Oedipal theme and the stasis of the 'split' theme, by developing the submerged 'artist' theme, which resolves the novel's contradictions and gives it a formal unity.

Although Paul possesses traits of sensitivity, introversion, observation and concentration which correspond to the stereotype of the artist, to some extent Paul the artist is, Maurice Beebe argues, a self-portrait of Lawrence. Paul's motivation comes first from his mother, and then from his muse, Miriam. The struggle between them therefore is 'not simply the vying of two women for Paul's love, but the jealous struggle of two patronesses for the homage of the artist and the right to control him' [*Casebook*, p. 181]. But all the women fail to realise the core of aloneness in Paul, which is the artist himself, and which they cannot share. Indeed, says Beebe, the main thesis in *Sons and Lovers* is that the artist's work is isolating and is something that can never be fully shared by women. Beebe regards Paul's art as extending beyond painting; enabling him to act out and resolve his Oedipal conflict by arranging the dramatic reconciliation between Clara and Baxter Dawes, and through the mercy killing of his mother to prepare for his creative rebirth. Like Stephen Dedalus on the strand, it is during a visit from his muse, Miriam, that Paul feels a new consecration to life and art; and just as Stephen shouts, 'Welcome, O life' at the end of *A Portrait of the Artist*, at the ambiguous conclusion of *Sons and Lovers* Paul turns his back on his past and makes for the town. Beebe comments 'Both Joyce and Lawrence conclude their portraits of the artist with the heroes, having tested and found wanting the claims of love and family, poised for exile, but an exile which is to lead to creative renewal' [*Casebook*, p. 189].

Maurice Beebe focuses on a narrow but interesting area of the novel and justifies his claim for the importance of the artist theme, and especially Paul's discovery of the artist's essential experience of isolation and detachment. However, his thesis is based on conjecture about the novel's origins and on the romantic idea of art as profoundly unconscious and inspirational, which he compares with Paul's experience of making love to Clara. While Beebe's attention to the influence of Miriam on Paul's artistic development is valuable, his treatment of Clara is less convincing. Moreover, his discussion misses the opportunity to explore the nature and value of Paul's artistic creed, and the claim that the artist theme unifies the novel cannot be fully substantiated. It may redeem the text from the schism imposed by the Freudian concerns of the 'split' theory, but Paul the artist grows up in and inhabits a historical community, and any account of his art must engage with his response to this society.

Genre criticism is at the opposite pole to psychoanalytical criticism in seeing the text, not as the unconscious revelation of the author's neuroses, but as a comparative study of artists writing within a conscious tradition. It is also far removed from the concern of historical criticism with the claims of the community. As a particular version of formalist criticism, its strengths lie in its endeavour to shift the emphasis away from a purely psychoanalytical view of character, in its revelation of formal patterns in the novel, and in the sharpness of perception offered by its thematic focus. However, there is a tendency to regard the hero, and indeed the other characters, as typical rather than individual; and, because the centre of interest is the development of the hero, the larger historical society within which he matures is effectively excluded. Most limiting, though, is the fact that the emphasis of genre criticism on pattern, clarity and unity is at the expense of complexity, contradiction and the ampler truth of realism.

Part Two:
Appraisal

Critical approach: liberal–humanist formalism

At the present time there is generally felt to be a crisis in English
studies, which, as Terry Eagleton has put it, constitutes a 'crisis
in the definition of the subject itself' [1983, p. 214]. For
Eagleton, literature should be treated as part of the whole field
of cultural studies, and similarly Peter Widdowson would like
to see a 're-siting of literature in history . . . as one specific
discourse in the general study of culture' [1982, p. 14]. This call
for a radical shift in the definition of literature and literary
criticism challenges the mainstream of liberal-humanist
criticism on the grounds that, in Terry Eagleton's words, it is
little more than a 'suburban moral ideology' [p. 207], out of
touch with the larger world of history, and political and cultural
studies. This book is not the place to enter the debate, but it is
against this background of a general revaluation of criticism as
an activity that the reader is invited to consider, along with the
other critical methodologies I have discussed, my own
approach to *Sons and Lovers*, which is perhaps best characterised
by the phrase 'liberal-humanist formalism', a widely held
critical position embracing a variety of kindred modes of
inquiry.

Although it is difficult to define briefly, liberal humanism is
essentially concerned with the central importance of human
happiness, with the potential for individual self-improvement,
and with mutual human responsibility. Its values therefore on
the whole tend to be private rather than public, and, because it
has to do with the individual's development of values through
the exercise of free will, liberal humanism is clearly
incompatible with all forms of determinism, such as Positivism

or Marxism. It is flexible, undogmatic and eschews narrow political or philosophical orthodoxy. For the liberal-humanist critic, this scepticism is also a method of inquiry, and he strives to retain a healthy suspicion of ideologies which offer sometimes incisive, but necessarily reductive, views of literary texts. Of course it will be readily recognised that this position is itself ideological, but it is an ideology that embodies a flexible, vigilant study of literature, endeavouring to understand the complexities of literary art and resisting the temptation of doctrinal certitude. Although I seek to incorporate in my examination of *Sons and Lovers* those insights made available by more specialised methodologies – for instance historicism or feminism – these are, like psychoanalysis, essentially branches of other disciplines, such as psychology, history, sociology or politics, rather than the proper domain of literary criticism.

What is strikingly absent from more overtly ideological criticism and from general cultural criticism is a serious consideration of the aesthetic properties of literary texts. Because in my view literary criticism should be concerned with, among other things, the quality of the writer's moral imagination as embodied in the text under discussion – with the artistic truthfulness of his writing – my critical approach focuses on the formal aspects of the novel, rather than on those facets of it revealed by the methodologies of, for instance, biography, psychoanalysis or history; for, although in their different ways these throw some light on the text's meaning, it is in the examination of its formal components that we can observe most clearly the author's imagination at work – his deepest artistic instinct as well as his conscious craftsmanship. The novel's structural patterns, which are composed of such features as narrative point of view, scenes, symbolism, parallels of characterisation, and language, are the writer's means of exploring, defining and objectifying the subject of his imagination. Of course in this sense several of the critical categories I have been examining in the first part of this book overlap to some extent with formalist criticism: source criticism, which elicits from *Sons and Lovers* an autobiographical pattern; the psychoanalytical approach, which sees in this novel the clear outline of a Freudian case study; historical analysis, which regards Paul's development as confirming the structure of bourgeois industrial capitalism; and genre criticism, which examines the pattern created by Lawrence's novel of education in the context of fiction sharing a similar concern. However, unlike a formalist approach, these particular schools of criticism bring to the study of *Sons and Lovers* certain preconceptions about its formal properties and hence about its meaning. The Marxist historical critic will be alert to identify Lawrence's own ideology and the way the novel embodies the structure of a class society; the psychoanalyst will be looking for patterns of behaviour confirming Paul's Oedipal development; while the genre critic will wish to know whether the novel fits into a particular species of fiction. Formalist criticism endeavours to be more open-minded and disinterested, and, in attending to the way the novel has been constructed, it discovers a greater degree of complexity in its form and meaning. Indeed, it was because Lawrence himself perceived that artistic truth was extraordinarily complex that he reacted so angrily to the psychoanalyst Alfred Kuttner's reduction of the truth of fiction to what Lawrence called a 'half lie', by imposing on it an exclusively Freudian structure.

However, as early New Criticism bears out, there is a danger in the kind of formalist approach which offers a single, simple unified view of *Sons and Lovers*, based on a classical sense of clarity and definition, and which analyses its formal constituents as if they were hermetically sealed from real experience. It is evident, for instance, in the narrowly formalist interpretation of Dorothy Van Ghent, which reads the novel as a symbolic poem. My own formalist approach is more flexible, and it follows also that as a liberal humanist I cannot endorse her approval of the individual's submission to the non-human life force, any more than I am able to agree with the opposite ideology, implicit in historical criticism, which sees the novel's form as in some sense historically determined, and the necessary submerging of the individual in the community. Form in *Sons and Lovers* represents Lawrence's endeavour imaginatively and truthfully to incorporate in fiction the complexity and muddle of the real world, and therefore critics' conception of form must include contradiction, ambiguity and inconclusiveness. Nor is form in this novel something divorced from the reader – life frozen into a frame for his contemplation. The act of writing is also Lawrence's attempt to persuade the reader of the reality and truth of his interpretation of experience, and it follows that certain aspects of the novel's form also possess this essentially rhetorical function. Our understanding of the function of form in *Sons and Lovers* must therefore include our sense of both its moral realism and its rhetoric. In this section of the book I examine the significance of particular formal qualities in *Sons and Lovers* about which critics are in dispute: the fundamental unity of the novel as offering a coherent view of life; its impersonal nature as a work of art; the highly conscious quality of Lawrence's craftsmanship; and finally the truthful complexity of the novel's form and meaning.

Lawrence himself defined the development of the form of *Sons and Lovers* as 'slow, like growth' [*Casebook*, p. 25], and, in spite of several critics' insistence to the contrary, so far as its unity is concerned the reader is not aware of any radical split between its psychological and social centres of interest, nor of any hiatus between what some critics have defined as the marvellous realism of the first half of the novel and the Freudian case study of the second part. These schisms really reflect the limiting effect of ideological criticism. Moreover, Lawrence's conscious craftsmanship and the impersonal nature of the novel are evident in his immaculate control of the narrative point of view. Most critics contend that Paul's view of experience dominates the novel and, moreover, that, because it is shared by Lawrence himself, it produces distorted portraits of the other characters. However, I seek to demonstrate that Paul's situation and development are treated with a high degree of artistic detachment and objectivity, by Lawrence's employment of multiple points of view which place his experience in perspective. The formal articulation of *Sons and Lovers* also depends to a large extent on Lawrence's craftsmanship in drawing on his abilities as a poet and dramatist. Critics who acknowledge the presence of formal elements deriving from these genres frequently choose to focus on one of them – showing either how the poetic symbolism serves a vitalistic interpretation of the novel, or alternatively, how the social realism of the scenes of conflict supports a historical view of the text. Of course these are polarised approaches, which do not reflect the great art with which Lawrence integrates both poetry and drama into his fiction in order to emphasise the fundamental interrelation of nature and society in human experience.

Organic unity: 'slow, like growth'

In the light of the history of *Sons and Lovers* criticism, it is important to insist on its artistic unity. A liberal-formalist reading of the novel must attend to the presentation of character in all its complexity; however, at one extreme of the critical spectrum *Sons and Lovers* is interpreted as an Oedipal novel, which records the inner working of its hero's and his creator's unconscious; while at the other extreme some critics offer a novel which is about a specifically realised historical society and one individual's attempt to locate himself within it. The psychological case study and the historical form which these interpretations suggest are not, however, mutually exclusive. This is so partly because the psychological and the historical were aspects of Lawrence's own experience of growing-up in the Eastwood community; but more importantly it is because as an artist Lawrence sought to reveal the whole truth about a complex human situation, by demonstrating the intimate interrelation between the unconscious and the historical; between the psychological and the social dimensions of experience. To a large extent this is where our sense of the unity of *Sons and Lovers* resides. The reader is involved emotionally with the inner life of Paul Morel through his Oedipal dependence on his mother and his frustrated efforts to free himself from her; but Paul is at the same time distanced from the reader to some degree by Lawrence's acute awareness of the enveloping social circumstances in which he is caught. Lawrence sees Paul's situation as both personally unique and also historically representative of the emergence after the Education Act of 1870 of a new educated working class. Although for Lawrence Paul's efforts at achieving his individual identity and establishing his fundamental artistic values are supremely important, they can only be fully understood in the historical context of the society in which the struggle takes place.

This continual interaction between the personal and the social is both a moral and a formal principle in *Sons and Lovers*. Paul's unnaturally close relationship with his mother explains why other relationships – with his father, with Miriam and with Clara – are extremely difficult for him to sustain; but the concretely realised mining community is also integral to Paul's whole experience, both as a man and as an artist. Every event of his young life is fraught with psychological, social and aesthetic implications for the growth of his character. One example of Lawrence's tactfully artistic treatment of this complexity, in a single minor, yet telling, incident, occurs when he and his mother set off for Willey Farm. Pausing to watch coal waste being tipped from waggons onto the great pit-hill, Paul decides to sketch the scene. His mother looks at the red cottages and the green landscape and responds to it with a rather bland enthusiasm:

> 'The world is a wonderful place,' she said, 'and wonderfully beautiful.'
> 'And so's the pit,' he said. 'Look how it heaps together, like something alive almost – a big creature that you don't know . . . But I like the feel of *men* on things, while they're alive. There's a feel of men about trucks, because they've been handled with men's hands, all of them.' [p. 167]

Mrs Morel reacts to Paul's strong emotional and artistic response shortly, steering the conversation away from the spell-binding mystery and humanity of the pit to a more rational discussion about the economic security represented by the lines of standing trucks, for, as she is well aware, Paul's assertion challenges her psychological and ideological need to dominate her son and mould his values. He proclaims, almost in passing, what is later confirmed in his conversation with her about working-class as opposed to middle-class values, in his sturdy defence of the coal pit at Bestwood in his discussions with Clara, and in his talk with her in Nottingham about the merits of the town – that his commitment as an individual and as an artist is to the pit, to the landscape shaped by human hands, and to the working-class community of his father – the ultimate source of his artistic values.

In the formation of Paul's character, the relation between the Oedipal element and his development of values that derive from his social experience is complex, and is by no means confined to the present. Early in the novel Lawrence indicates briefly and deftly the way that both Oedipal and class influences, modifying and reinforcing each other, may be mediated through the generations. There is a hint of something akin to an Electra complex in Mrs Morel's love–hate relationship with her handsome father, which is underscored by Lawrence's statement that her father 'was to her the type of all men' [p. 44], just as she becomes for Paul the type of all women. We also learn that George Coppard was an ascetic, puritanical, overbearing and ironic man, who was closest in sympathy to the Apostle Paul. At first Gertrude Coppard tried to reproduce this relationship with the respectable son of a well-to-do tradesman, who wanted to enter the Church, but when this love affair failed she escaped her father's influence by marrying the sensual, carefree young miner, from a different class and a different world. And it is this pattern that is repeated in Paul's own relationships with the intensely religious Miriam and the sensual, worldly Clara, as he seeks to escape his mother's claustrophobic love. However, its neurotic nature is not in itself sufficient cause to account for his particular personal and artistic development. This also depends on his mother's endeavour to inculcate in him moral and social values which stem from the Protestant individualism of her revered father, an engineer, and her grandfather, who had been a lace-manufacturer. She offers Paul the bourgeois inheritance that she had rejected, and her intense longing for her son's social success is a measure of her own bitterly frustrated life. She frankly wants him to marry a lady and she urges him, as she had urged William before him, to climb up into the world of the middle class.

Mrs Morel's bourgeois values encompass self-help, the work ethic, respectability and the sanctity of the life of the mind, all of which she has applied with inflexible righteousness to her husband. She is estranged from him by her religious faith, her individualist ideology and her bourgeois command of language; and she consciously strives to nurture in Paul an aversion to his father's way of life; to the brute physicality and danger of pit labour and more generally to what she regards as the pervasive atmosphere of cultural despair – the dirt, the drinking, the degradation and waste. The effect of this on Paul is intensified by the fact that Mrs Morel is the focus of social change for her children, as Lawrence shows the pit community itself being disturbed by new rhythms of internal contradiction, which come from the wider world beyond Bestwood. While the miners value traditional male supremacy and a collective solidarity based on the pit and the public house, the women who have joined the Women's Guild seek to improve the quality of their cramped lives. As one of its leading figures, Mrs

Morel gains enhanced status in her children's eyes. Yet her social aspirations are not only political, but also intensely personal, for in seeking to transcend the working-class community through her children, she is also striving to redeem the failure of her married life. Young Paul Morel is thus the focus of a multitude of forces – Oedipal, social and historical – which combine to weigh increasingly on his developing artistic sensibility.

A similarly complex interrelation of the psychological and the historical is evident in the character and function of Walter Morel, who represents more than simply Paul's ogre-like Oedipal rival. More than any other figure in *Sons and Lovers*, he stands for the norms and values of the mining community. Although he is strongly individualised, so that he is always much more than a typical figure, he is a representative miner in several important respects. He lacks education, is almost illiterate and insists on the physical authority, the exclusiveness and solidarity of traditional masculine working-class society. His inarticulateness and his dialect separate him from his family, as does his frequent absence at the public house, and his shortness of temper, brought on by physical exhaustion. And, in his attempts to assert his traditional authority as father and head of the household against the effective usurpation of this role by his superior wife, Morel continually allows himself to be goaded into clumsily aggressive actions, which alienate him still further from his children. Paul's initial rejection of his father's values, therefore, has as much to do with class and gender conflict within the family as it does with his unconscious Oedipal rivalry with his father for his mother's affections; as is evident in the rift between the parents over Morel's deceit about the rent, the occasion of the cropping of William's hair, the row over the visit of the clergyman, the theft of Mrs Morel's sixpence, and Morel's sociable drinking with his fellow miners.

It would be a mistake, however, to interpret Paul's turning from his father, as some critics have, as inseparable from his rejection of the poverty-stricken and oppressive world of the colliery for the emancipated sphere of the mind; for it is neither a complete nor a permanent turning-away either from his father or from the pit community and the world of work. Far from fearing reabsorption into the working class, Paul later explicitly rejects middle-class values for those of his father's

people, and in his choice of a career as a commercial artist he is
by no means seeking to abandon the world of production for the
life of the mind, or of the aesthetic sensibility. As an artist Paul
longs for a sense of the wholeness of life, and this includes the
absolute centrality of the pit in his experience, almost as a
religious presence – a metaphysical validation of social reality.
When Clara is repelled by the coal pit rising still and black
among the cornfields, Paul responds,

> 'You see, I am so used to it I should miss it. No; and I like the pits here and
> there. I like the rows of trucks, and the headstocks, and the steam in the
> daytime, and the lights at night. When I was a boy, I always thought a
> pillar of cloud by day and a pillar of fire by night was a pit, with its steam,
> and its lights, and the burning bank, – and I thought the Lord was always
> at the pit-top.' (p. 384)

The interrelation of Oedipal and class influences in Paul's
experience is one aspect of Lawrence's comprehensive realism
in *Sons and Lovers*. Another important dimension is his
awareness of the way that relationships are partly defined by
economics as well as by psychology. At the level of realistic
background detail, money is a pervasive influence in the novel.
We learn how close to poverty the mining families live, the
effects of the pits shutting down at intervals during periods of
slack demand in the summer, the arrangements for sick pay, the
way wives supplement the family income by seaming stockings,
Clara Dawes's sweated labour at lace-making, the penny-
pinching to buy a little treat on market days, and scenes such as
Morel's sharing-out the week's earnings in the back kitchen –
all of which reinforce our sense of the basic economic reality of
life in a pit village. Like other relationships in the community,
Paul's love for his mother is forged and sustained in the context
of money. Their moments of flirtation as 'lovers' involve buying
a cheap pot at the market, delighting in the prize money that
Paul wins for his painting, worrying over the bill at the tea shop,
and admiring the inexpensive but smart blouse that Mrs Morel
buys herself. In this way Paul becomes a surrogate husband,
sharing with his mother all the little financial anxieties and
triumphs that his father has forfeited. And, unlike his father, or
William, when Paul gets a job he gives all his income to his
mother, which in effect signals the removal of his father from his
position as the centre of the household. However, if economics

contributes obliquely to the growth of this Oedipal relationship, it also assists in sowing the seeds of its dissolution. Clara Dawes is attractive to Paul as a symbol of the new woman, who asserts not only her sexual, but also her economic, independence, and it is this combination of economic as well as psychological and sexual liberation that makes Paul feel even more intensely the claustrophobic nature of his relationship with his mother, and seek to free himself.

For some critics *Sons and Lovers* is not a unified novel, not because of a hiatus between its psychological and its social concerns, but because it displays a basic formal weakness. The first half is seen as offering a deeply felt naturalistic study of working-class life in a Midlands pit community, while the second half is regarded as being wholly concerned with Paul's adolescent psychological development and his relations with his parents, with Miriam and with Clara. This is a view shared by critics who approach the novel from different perspectives. For John Worthen, Lawrence's Oedipal idea takes over in the 'Strife in Love' chapter; Scott Sanders sees Paul's gradual ideological formation being followed necessarily by his alienation from his community; in more formal terms Frank O'Connor regards *Sons and Lovers* as commencing as a classical nineteenth-century realist text and ending as a modern one; and Jerome Buckley argues that the second half turns into a Freudian case history, with an accompanying change in style from dramatisation and description to extensive analysis.

Some of these views are the result of ideological preoccupations; others are impressionistic judgements. For instance, so far as style is concerned, in fact one half of *Sons and Lovers* is in the form of dialogue, which predominates in its central sections, both the early and the concluding chapters being more descriptive and analytical. Equally subjective is the view that the realistic study of the mining village is abruptly replaced in the second half of the novel by an exclusive focus on Paul's consciousness. In fact, from Paul's birth and his earliest relationship with his mother, Lawrence signals his intention of concentrating the narrative interest on him, as for instance in those symbolic scenes in which Mrs Morel dedicates the baby Paul to the sun, and in which the blood from his mother's wound seeps into his scalp. In the early part of the novel Lawrence is concerned with tracing the effects on Paul's consciousness of his environment, but more subtly he is also concerned to define the way the lives of previous generations effectively limit the freedom of action of individuals in the present. Lawrence's view of Paul's Oedipal fixation as part of a pattern of cause and effect – reaching back into the past and his mother's relationship with her father, and stretching forward into Paul's future relationships with women – is crucially established by the end of the first part of the novel, when Paul falls ill after William's death, and his desperate appeal to his mother for love and life leads to her claiming him as William's replacement. Moreover, William's death early in the novel, hastened by overwork as he strives to secure a place in the middle class and please his mother, enables us better to comprehend the later clash of imperatives within Paul's mature consciousness as he struggles to choose between the working class and the middle class; between the collective and the individual. From an early age Paul is alive to the increasingly powerful necessity of choosing between these two sets of values, which contributes to his neuroticism. The environment of the community affects him not only directly through contact with the mine, with his father's friends, and with the neighbours, but more subtly and powerfully through his parents, whose battle between the values of pit and public house on the one hand, and of chapel and Women's Guild on the other, is partly class warfare. And Paul's choice of his father's values towards the end of the novel stems directly from his allegiance to the mining community established in the first half of the book, symbolised by the almost metaphysical presence of the pit in his young consciousness, as he affirms to his mother his preference for the vitality and solidarity of his father's people, rather than the arid intellectualism of the middle class: 'the difference between people isn't in their class, but in themselves. Only from the middle classes one gets ideas, and from the common people – life itself, warmth' (p. 315).

The commencement of the second half of the novel is not registered by any sudden change of narrative focus or style – as Lawrence said, the development of *Sons and Lovers* is organic, 'slow, like growth' (*Casebook*, p. 25) – but rather he presents with artistic tact the growth of Paul's character as he enters adolescence, becomes more self-absorbed, falls in love with Miriam, gets a job in Nottingham and broadens his social horizons through visits to the theatre, and socialist discussion groups. For what gives *Sons and Lovers* its fundamental organic unity is the fact that it is concerned with the education into life of an artist for whom choices are always crucially important, and whose developing consciousness becomes more interesting as he matures. Thus his early Oedipal rivalry with his father is later complicated by his ambiguous experience with a father figure in Baxter Dawes. Moreover, his artistic awareness of what he calls a 'fourth dimension' of experience – which he could not articulate as a child, then locates within nature, and finally discovers within the community – deepens as he moves towards his twin Oedipal and cultural crises. Their resolution is triggered by the convergence of the novel's two plots – Paul's relationship with his parents, and his involvement in another triangular relationship with Clara and Baxter Dawes – which come to a climax at the same time. Effectively they are the same crisis, for freedom from the emancipated modernity of Clara, and from the competitive individualism of his mother, involves embracing the masculine working-class values of his father and Baxter Dawes.

Artistic impersonality: narrative point of view

Counterbalancing Lawrence's statement that 'one sheds one's sicknesses in books' (*Casebook*, p. 26), is his equally confident assertion that in *Sons and Lovers* he was deliberately aiming to write a 'restrained, somewhat impersonal novel' [*Casebook*, p. 21]. There has been a tendency in Lawrence criticism to prefer the former statement. Terry Eagleton, for instance, argues that what the psychoanalytical school of criticism reveals is the novel's sub-text, in which Lawrence's unconscious meanings are laid bare by certain points of ambiguity (Paul's love–hate relationship with his father), evasion (Paul cannot face the truth about the way his father's industrial world is shaping his life), overemphasis (the bold authorial assertion that Walter Morel had 'denied the God in him' – p. 102), and suppression (Paul is never permitted to express his bitterness at his mother's possessiveness). This unconscious pattern, it is argued, is reinforced formally by the way in which Lawrence structured the novel from Paul's point of view, which in effect constitutes a conspiracy between the author's unconscious motivation (arising from a combination of psychological and social factors in Lawrence's own experience) and his artistic arrangement of his material. The evidence offered in support of this view is the way the novel seemingly tells us one thing, but shows us another. H.M. Daleski, for instance [*Casebook*, pp. 191–207] draws attention to the way that Lawrence's emphatic and apparently irrevocable condemnation of Walter Morel is contradicted by those scenes which serve to demonstrate his spontaneous vitality and warmth. However, it is erroneous to make the assumption that it is Paul's point of view that carries the burden of Lawrence's overt meaning, while the dramatised scenes are in some way the product of his unconscious sympathies. Indeed, this seemingly inartistic hiatus between 'telling' and 'showing', which occurs at key junctures in the narrative, is an important formal principle and the product of Lawrence's deliberate artistic choice. The kind of psychoanalytical criticism referred to by Terry Eagleton is unduly influenced by the autobiographical origins of Lawrence's material, by the critics' stress on his adoption of the hero's point of view as a central feature of the narrative design, and by a belief in the tyranny of the unconscious over the processes of Lawrence's imagination. Critics who interpret the novel solely from Paul's point of view tend to regard Mrs Morel as a long-suffering victim of marital oppression, Walter Morel as a brutalised drunkard and Miriam as a nun-like figure; but the novel as a whole eschews these psychological and social stereotypes in favour of an infinitely more complex view of character.

Sons and Lovers is the product of a highly conscious art. However, Lawrence's endeavour to transform autobiography into the impersonality of art is not, to be sure, the impersonality of the artist paring his fingernails in detached contemplation behind his work of art, as James Joyce put it, for Lawrence was very passionately involved with his novels. Rather it is the employment of the novel's formal elements in such a way as to achieve a balanced account of reality and to communicate this through a rhetoric composed of both sympathy and irony – sympathy drawing the reader close to the characters in a compassionate understanding of their situation, irony distancing him at the same time in moral judgement. This is achieved not only through the balanced use of 'telling' and 'showing', but also through Lawrence's sophisticated control of the narrative point of view. In *Sons and Lovers* he portrays the gestation of the soul of an artist from early childhood, and our sympathy is engaged for Paul from the beginning, by his being the sensitive child of an unhappy marriage, by his early identification as the hero of the story and therefore deserving of our particular attention, and by the fact that we are immediately immersed in his consciousness. However, a simultaneous distancing-effect is achieved by the simple irony of Paul's development being described from the point of view of the author in the present. Thus there are effectively two major narrative points of view in the novel: that of the child, whose response to experience is faithfully recorded, and that of the implied author, the book's main narrative voice (who should not be confused with the historical D.H. Lawrence), which places Paul's experience in a fuller and clearer perspective. However, the relationship between the hero, the author and the reader is rendered more complex by the fact that it alters as the hero develops. As he grows to adulthood, Paul is increasingly exposed to the author's explicit moral judgement. At the same time, however, the change in narrative tone required to register his mature consciousness leads to a closer identification of implied author, hero and reader. And yet our sympathy for Paul is also qualified throughout by the ironic perspectives offered by the judgements of other important characters, such as his mother, Miriam and Clara, creating a subtly balanced account of Paul's moral nature.

Our sympathy is evoked most strongly for Paul in the early part of *Sons and Lovers*, and particularly in the chapter 'The Young Life of Paul', in which Lawrence presents a series of typical scenes from his childhood – his parents' battles; his love for his mother and hatred for his father; his father's domestic life (making fuses, telling stories and bullying the family); blackberrying for his mother in coppices and quarries; collecting his father's wages from the offices of the coal company; scouring the market for bargains with his mother – in which Lawrence develops our awareness of Paul's unnatural dependence on his mother. However, even in these early sections of the novel, Paul is not treated without irony. His extreme sensitivity and sense of alienation from his father's community are revealed sympathetically when he visits the pay-room of the coal company, but also in evidence is his snobbery, which contributes to what his mother calls his 'ridiculous hypersensitiveness' [pp. 112–13]. And later he is similarly tortured by this sense of class difference when he is looking for job advertisements in the reading-room of the public library, where he believes people are judging him for his moral degradation in living at home with his mother instead of going down the pit.

In spite of our sympathy for Paul's suffering on his mother's behalf, Lawrence does not permit his view of his father to stand unqualified. Paul's judgement of him as a brutal, careless, inarticulate drunkard is counterbalanced and placed in an ironic perspective by the more objective description and dramatisation of scenes in which Morel's warmth, humour, tenderness, delight in creative activity and capacity to spin yarns make him the vital centre of family life. And later, when Paul sells a painting, in the middle of the family celebration we find, with a sense of tender shock, Morel weeping for his dead son, William. Moreover, we are made aware that in his own way Morel really cares for his wife, bringing her tea in bed (only to be scolded in case it has no sugar), and this tenderness emerges again at her death, though he is also frightened and awkward, feeling pushed to one side by his son. Lawrence's treatment of Morel is a good deal more sympathetic than those critics who accord priority to Paul's point of view have noted, and, although Morel is gradually pushed into the background of the story by the narrative focus on Paul, he never loses our sympathy – nor are we therefore greatly surprised when Paul finally turns not to the grave, nor to the pastoral retreat that the idyllic Miriam episode might suggest, but back towards the town and the common world of work, of vitality and spontaneous feeling, which his father has come to represent.

Those psychoanalytical and feminist critics who approach Paul's relationship with Miriam from Paul's point of view, believing it to be endorsed by Lawrence's sympathy for his hero, focus on Miriam's function in Paul's Oedipal situation as the rival to his mother, and on his brutal treatment of her – for instance, when he criticises her intense love for Hubert, harangues her over her tremulous fear of mathematics, and imposes himself on her sexually. However, the author's attitude to Paul's cruelty in fact distances the reader in judgement, as

Paul is condemned both from his own mouth and from the author's explicit commentary. A degree of self-condemnation is apparent when Mrs Leivers asks Paul not to be so hard on Miriam: "'I can't help it," he said rather pitiably. "I go off like it"' (p. 207). And the author makes a severe judgement of Paul's moral myopia in believing that his friendship with Miriam is merely platonic: 'He was a fool who did not know what was happening to himself' (p. 224). Lawrence never lets us see Paul bullying or humiliating Miriam without making us feel exactly where he is going wrong morally, and he continually reminds us of Paul's capacity for self-deception.

Ironically, the collapse of their relationship occurs in the spring, a time of sexual awakening, when Miriam's instinctual celebration both of the season and of their love, arouses Paul's ill humour, as they quarrel over her intense joy in the flowers. And Paul's contribution to the failure of their love affair, as the author makes clear, is partly through his insensitivity during their love-making. He is hurt that she has not been with him during their union, but the reader is made aware that neither has Paul: 'He had always, almost wilfully, to put her out of count, and act from the brute strength of his own feelings. And he could not do it often, and there remained afterwards always the sense of failure and of death' (p. 352). We are made to understand the extent of Paul's self-deception in rationalising this failure, his cynicism in blaming Miriam and, to his mother's astonishment, his forgetting her in a bout of drinking. However, this view is encompassed by Lawrence's larger sympathy for both Miriam and Paul. Miriam feels that the failure of their love is the result of Mrs Morel's tyrannical hold over her son's affections; Paul sees it as Miriam's need to possess him and his feelings completely. Although both are true, even taken together they are an incomplete version of the truth, because the reader also has to take account of, on the one hand, Miriam's religiosity, which offends Paul, and her fear of sexual relations, which he finds distressing; and, on the other hand, Paul's social snobbery, artistic hypersensitivity and melancholia. The whole truth, Lawrence suggests, is muddled. Far from sympathising with Paul at the expense of Miriam, Lawrence's treatment of both the young lovers displays a sympathy which envelopes the uniquely complex yet typical situation in which they find themselves, so that their adolescent relationship is handled with a tenderness and an honesty that compels the reader's assent.

One of the ways in which the reader's sympathy for Paul Morel is carefully qualified is by his predictability. The reader can almost anticipate – with his practised sense of the common pattern of sexual and social initiation belonging to the *Bildungsroman* – Paul's inevitable lurching from Miriam to her extreme opposite, Clara, from the shy, intense, virginal, religious girl to the voluptuous, sexually experienced woman of the world, although in the process Paul becomes a dissociated and self-divided individual, for, unlike his relationship with Miriam, his affair with Clara involves revealing little of his inner emotional life. Clara's own view of Paul is a further important means by which Lawrence distances us from him and places his experience of their relationship in an ironic light. For Paul his first sexual encounter with Clara, which counterpoints his strained, guilt-ridden love-making with Miriam, is a profound initiation into a new mode of being, and he feels at one with the universe. For Clara, however, older than Paul, a woman, and married, the development of their love affair is less clear and its possible resolution ambivalent. Moreover, Mrs Morel's view of the relationship – that Clara does not pose a threat to herself because she is not secure in Paul's affection, and also lacks either the temperament or the intellect to hold him – is sufficiently complacent to make us feel that it has no real chance of permanence: 'But you'll tire of her, my son; you know you will' (p. 394). Miriam, too, corroborates this sense of the temporary nature of the love between Paul and Clara in her judgement that Paul's feeling for Clara is 'shallow and temporal' (p. 336). All these different points of view conspire to undermine Paul's ecstatic response to his new love affair and distance the reader in compassionate judgement on his self-deception.

Ironically, Clara offers Paul the opportunity to release himself from the web of self-delusion in which he is enmeshed. She comes to him from the adult world of work, marriage and politics, and with the potential, through her independence of judgement, to stimulate him into self-appraisal. For instance, she sees his entanglement with Miriam in a very different light from the way he sees it. Instead of regarding Miriam's love as suffocating and suffused with religious worship, she discerns a normal, healthily possessive love, the kind that she herself comes to feel that Paul is unable to give, and she tells him in very plain terms that Miriam 'doesn't want any of your soul communion. That's your own imagination. She wants you' (p. 338). Clara's point of view opens up fresh perspectives on Paul, for she finds him lacking, not only as a man, but as an artist, flawed by his overactive imagination and innate predilection for self-serving distortion. And, although she is no art critic, and is unrepentantly dogmatic, there is, as Paul angrily concedes, an element of truth in such critical remarks as, 'You are affected in that piece' (p. 323). Clara's point of view is employed by Lawrence as a further corrective to our sympathy for the novel's hero, as he is judged and found wanting by an independent and mature woman who loves him. Moreover, her judgement of Paul's dangerously naïve self-absorption is corroborated by Lawrence's introduction of a broader authorial view, which places Paul's own analysis of his relationship to both Miriam and Clara in a severely ironic perspective: 'He saw none of the anomaly of his position. Miriam was his old friend, lover, and she belonged to Bestwood and home and his youth. Clara was a newer friend, and she belonged to Nottingham, to life, to the world. It seemed to him quite plain' (p. 336). Paul's point of view is by no means the only one, then, in *Sons and Lovers*. His version of the truth of his story is centrally important and a crucial means of gaining sympathy for him, but it is endlessly qualified by other competing perspectives, and in control of these viewpoints is the implied author, who is concerned throughout to testify to the complexity of the truth.

Lawrence's control of the pattern of sympathy and irony, closeness and distance, also extends to the other main characters, particularly Walter Morel, and is achieved in various ways. One method is the combination of dialogue and authorial statement. The tense family conference, when Morel has a dangerous accident at the pit and is critically ill, reveals a strong vein of selfishness in Mrs Morel's sympathy. She is anxious about him, but her natural compassion is tempered by her depression at this further confirmation, brought about by the crisis, that she does not truly love her husband, and also by the practical nuisance that hospital-visiting and convalescence involve – a feeling in which the children are all implicated, as the author summarises the family's response to near tragedy: 'They learned how perfectly peaceful the home could be. And they almost regretted – though none of them would have owned to such callousness – that their father was soon coming back' (p. 129). Although sympathetic to those emotional and practical difficulties of Mrs Morel which the dialogue reveals, the author is fairly explicit in his judgement of the family's desire to exclude Morel from his natural rights of love and home.

The subtlety of Lawrence's control of the narrative point of view is also evident within individual scenes. In that fraught encounter in which Morel incurs his wife's fury for cutting William's hair, we are made aware of the complex reverberations of an apparently trivial domestic row. It serves to register the intensity of Mrs Morel's possessive love for her children and the clumsy nature of Morel's own affections; it indicates how the children are to become instruments in the battle of wills between them; and it also reveals the ideological division within the marriage – Morel feels that his son is being made to look effeminate and he wants to assert the norms of the mining community (it is significant that he later endearingly calls his baby third son, Arthur, his 'little collier' (p. 86). Although throughout this scene we occupy Mrs Morel's point of view as she discovers the sacrilege and confronts her startled husband, our sympathy is really with Walter Morel. We feel that he has as much right as she has to decide when the baby's hair will be cut; that his desire to observe social convention is not unreasonable; and that his wife's overreaction is made to seem tragically absurd by his stunned silence – a judgement which is later confirmed by her admission that she has been silly. And the reader's refusal of sympathy is endorsed by her response to this event, at a deeper level, as the turning-point in her relationship with her husband, regarding him ever afterwards as an outsider, and revealing a bitter intransigence at the core of her nature.

Sympathy for Morel is also achieved through Lawrence's employment of an ironic perspective in that poignant scene when he arrives home from work on the day of Paul's birth. It is a scene which involves the reversal of both Mrs Morel's and the reader's expectations. At first Lawrence employs her point of view to register her bitterness at her husband's lateness in returning from the public house, which confirms his lack of love and care for her and for her new child. Ironically, and symbolic of his whole working life, he has been hammering futilely to clear intractable rock in his poor stall. The measure of sympathy thus gained for Morel increases when he returns home exhausted and irritable to be confronted by Mrs Bower, who invokes her female solidarity with his oppressed wife and treats him with scarcely concealed contempt. And, when he finally greets his wife, the author gives a truthfully realistic judgement of his state of mind without diminishing our sympathy: 'He stood at a loss what to say next. He was tired, and this bother was rather a nuisance to him, and he didn't quite know where he was' (p. 69). Sympathy and irony are inextricably linked in the conclusion to this scene. The parents want to kiss each other in celebration of their child's safe arrival, but neither dares make a sign, and so this fragile moment of opportunity for some kind of reconciliation passes.

Lawrence's use of the narrative point of view leads to a different kind of emotional equilibrium in the scene dealing with the visit of the Congregational minister, Mr Heaton. Initially the point of view switches from Mrs Morel and the young clergyman, who are made to feel somewhat guilty by Morel's early arrival home from work to interrupt their genteel afternoon tea, to Morel, who, feeling ill-tempered and threatened by their middle-class security and manners, plays the role of the boorish miner and forces on Mr Heaton's attention the dirty, sweaty reality of manual labour. Mrs Morel is sarcastic at her husband's disregard of her clean tablecloth, while William hates his father's false sentiment and disrespect for his mother and her friends. Each of these different points of view conveys its own partial truth about the embarrassing situation, which ends in farcical confusion as the parents quarrel, the baby cries, Annie (who has been accidentally struck on the head by a saucepan) whines and William, in the midst of the bedlam, sarcastically intones from the text above the mantlepiece, 'God Bless Our Home!' (p. 72), at which Mrs Morel collapses in hysterical laughter. The scene appropriately ends in comic equilibrium, which subsumes the reader's contrary impulses to sympathise and to judge, and which embodies characteristically Lawrence's enveloping sympathy for the bitter frustration of each of the participants, for beneath its comic rhythm there is an underlying human misery.

Craftsmanship: drama and poetry

Most criticism of *Sons and Lovers* focuses quite properly on its
narrative chronology – on Paul's psychological odyssey, on his
growth as an artist, or on his alienation from his working-class
roots. However, by attending to Lawrence's conscious
craftsmanship (in so far as this can be usefully distinguished
from the more embracing concept of his art) – and in particular
by examining his employment of the expressive modes of poetry
and drama – formalist criticism facilitates a fuller understanding of those significant points in the novel where Lawrence's use
of form transcends the linear narrative. These are events, or
moments, which alert the reader to the simultaneous
manifestation in human experience of the social and the
spiritual, the communal and the natural, or the real and the
ideal. Critics of *Sons and Lovers* have tended to treat Lawrence's
employment of the genres of poetry and drama separately;
regarding his social realism as being rendered essentially in his
detailed descriptions of Bestwood and in his dramatisation of
personal and class conflict, while his vitalistic philosophy is
embodied in his poetic use of patterns of imagery. However,
with great craft Lawrence brings together these very different
formal elements in *Sons and Lovers*, creating a dynamic interplay
between them, in order to explore the characters' responses to
the opportunities that life proffers them to grasp a sense of the
wholeness of experience.

In the scene in which Mrs Morel, pregnant with Paul, is
locked out of the house by her husband, Lawrence transforms a
sordid domestic episode into something strangely powerful
through his employment of symbolism. However, although
Dorothy Van Ghent reads this scene as a symbolic, vitalistic
'set piece', Lawrence insists on the continuity of human
experience and is concerned to relate it to the tragic conflict of
the Morels' marriage. This integration of experience is
achieved by using in succession a narrative summary, with
balanced points of view; dramatic dialogue; and a symbolic
setting. The author records how, as a summertime holiday
jaunt, Morel and his friend Jerry Purdy walk over to
Nottingham, play skittles there with fellow miners, before
calling in at the Nelson public house on the way home; while
pregnant and wearied by the heat, his wife takes the children

down to the river, where Annie is irritating and William is in danger of drowning himself. Both points of view are given with scrupulous impartiality and our sympathy is evenly divided, for Morel's hard-earned day of heady freedom and male solidarity is counterbalanced by Mrs Morel's sense of sexual oppression and social imprisonment. Her pent-up resentment and his bad conscience quickly turn into a dramatic struggle over gender and class rights when he comes home, and she challenges his authority, provoking the response at the climax of the battle, 'It's me as brings th' money whoam, not thee. It's my house, not thine. Then ger out on't – ger out on't!' (p. 58). As she has effectively excluded him from her life, at this crisis he reacts by shutting her out from his home.

In the garden Mrs Morel's anger and anxiety are gradually assuaged by the mysterious otherness of the familiar setting transfigured by the moonlight. However, just as she refuses to acknowledge the social norms of the mining community, so she also denies the instinctual wholeness of experience which the world of nature offers (ironically, since she is pregnant – which affords her a grim smile when she later finds her face smudged with pollen). This is not a dream garden, but recognisably the little plot of a collier's house, with a corncrake calling and men's voices in the distance, for Lawrence's symbols are always rooted in concrete reality. However, although the moonlight suggests Mrs Morel's femininity, together with the white lilies it also symbolises her severe emotional chastity. She feels 'forlorn' in the 'mysterious out-of-doors' (p. 60), and the reader is invited to contrast this with the carefree instinct of her husband, who on his ramble simply fell asleep under an oak. While Morel's refusal of wholeness is represented in the quarrel scene by his assertion of communal rather than individual values, his wife's is registered by this suppression of her instinctual feelings. While the dramatised social context prompts our sympathy for both of these people trapped in their own history, the poetic context of nature underlines the inadequacy of Mrs Morel's imaginative response, not just to the collective life of the pit village, but also to the encompassing natural world.

This scene in the garden has its parallel later in the novel, when Paul decides to break with Miriam. Initially Paul is indoors, painting almost automatically as a way of escaping his dilemma, while his mother sits musing on his situation. There is a tense silence, for neither will speak out – he dreads the impending decision, and she wants him to separate freely from Miriam, but only in order that she may have him for herself. Paul's release comes in the garden, where 'the beauty of the night made him want to shout' (p. 355). As before, this ordinary garden possesses that almost tangible presence which had awed and repelled his mother, evoked once again by the 'scent of madonna lilies, almost as if it were prowling abroad' (p. 355). Lured out of doors by the clashing perfumes of the flowers, Paul is intoxicated, particularly by the coarse scent of the iris, which stands 'stiff in the darkness' (p. 356); and then he breaks off a pink and goes indoors, announcing his intention to end his love affair with Miriam. This episode modulates tactfully between psychological realism and sexual symbolism. The domesti- cated pink, which Paul breaks off, represents Miriam; the madonna lily, whose strong perfume competes with that of the other flowers, stands for his mother; while the purple phallic iris symbolises the sexual power of Clara. However, the distancing irony of this scene resides in its being framed by Mrs Morel's point of view, which alerts us to the fact that, although Paul's agonising decision is an overtly spontaneous act of will in response to the natural life force flowing through him, in truth his finishing with Miriam was entirely predictable, and clearly in effect freeing himself for Clara really means freeing himself for his mother. And this return to his mother is summarised by Lawrence's drawing together the flower symbolism with the dramatic and psychological realism of intimate domestic ritual: '"On Sunday I break off," he said, smelling the pink. He put the flower in his mouth. Unthinking, he bared his teeth, closed them on the blossom slowly, and had a mouthful of petals. These he spat into the fire, kissed his mother, and went to bed' (p. 356).

Lawrence's subtle juxtaposition of the familiar details of domestic life with a symbolic treatment of the natural world is used to emphasise both the overwhelming importance to Paul, and yet the inadequacy also, of his relationships with his mother and with Miriam. In the earlier 'Lad-and-Girl Love' chapter, Lawrence describes the creative communion that exists between Paul sketching and his mother sitting in her rocking-chair. It is normal experience heightened in a moment of relaxed happiness, with a strong Oedipal undercurrent: 'And he, with all his soul's intensity directing his pencil, could feel her warmth inside him like strength. They were both very happy so, and both unconscious of it. These times, that meant so much, and which were real living, they almost ignored' (p. 208). But Paul also needs Miriam in order to develop his critical insight into his work: 'From his mother he drew the life-warmth, the strength to produce; Miriam urged this warmth into intensity like a white light' (p. 208). The parallel between the relationships is loosely placed in time, but related in the text by juxtaposition, in order to emphasise the irony. Just as the presence of Mrs Morel energises Paul's art, so the creative magic of his presence can transfigure nature for Miriam: 'She wanted to show him a certain wild-rose bush she had discovered. She knew it was wonderful. And yet, till he had seen it, she felt it had not come into her soul. Only he could make it her own, immortal' (p. 209). For her this is primarily a religious moment, but Paul's more limited sexual response involves a sense of claustrophobia, as he runs breathlessly from the 'white, virgin scent' of the ivory roses and into the open air beyond the wood (p. 210). Lawrence draws our attention not just to the contrary claims and complementary functions of the two women in Paul's artistic life, but also to his failure to understand that these relationships offer him knowledge of the power of profound human communion to transform the ordinary world, and an intimation of the transcendent wholeness of experience that he seeks.

Lawrence's poetic symbolism can never be studied apart from the specific dramatic context within which it operates. A good example of the formal subtlety of Lawrence's craft is the episode in which Miriam infuriates Paul by caressing daffodils. Several critics, following Dorothy Van Ghent, have assumed that Paul's point of view is identical with that of the author, and have argued that Lawrence's symbolic treatment of the way Miriam cherishes the flowers is intended to reveal her blasphemous desire to possess and consume, not only the daffodils, but Paul as well. A more flexible formalist approach to this episode, however, attends carefully to its entire context – its dramatic realism and poetic symbolism, together with its changing narrative point of view, its balance of sympathy and judgement, and the contribution of the Oedipal pattern – and what emerges is a compelling artistic statement.

This episode demands to be seen as part of a larger emotional rhythm in the novel – Paul's return from Miriam to his mother – which spans three crucial days in his life. On the Friday evening of the loaf-burning incident, there is Mrs Morel's stunning revelation to Paul that she has never really had a husband, Paul's nakedly Oedipal confrontation with his father, and the first intimation of his mother's illness. This is followed by Paul's embarrassment on the Saturday morning, when Morel clumsily attempts a reconciliation with his son. So it is in a mood of bitterness and turmoil that Paul goes over to Willey Farm to meet Miriam on the Sunday. Reeling from the emotional onslaught at home, and under the impact of his renewed commitment to his mother, Paul feels that Miriam is curiously insubstantial. And yet at the same time, with her attractive new blouse, she represents to his thwarted sexual instinct the springtime world of growth and identity that he is giving up. His angrily iconoclastic mood, captured by his wicked parody of the Primitive Methodists' service, for the amusement of the Leivers family, extends to Miriam, the daffodils and nature itself:

> The cheeks of the flowers were greenish with cold. But still some had burst, and their gold ruffled and glowed. Miriam went on her knees before one cluster, took a wild-looking daffodil between her hands, turned up its face of gold to her, and bowed down, caressing it with her mouth and cheeks and brow. He stood aside, with his hands in his pockets, watching her. One after another she turned up to him the faces of the yellow, bursten flowers appealingly, fondling them lavishly all the while.
>   'Aren't they magnificent? she murmured.
>   'Magnificent! it's a bit thick – they're pretty!'   (p. 273)

Normally Paul's instinctual response would have been identical with Miriam's. Only a little later in the novel, when he is walking in the fields with Miriam and Clara, we are told that Paul wanted to drink the golden cowslips and chewed their little trumpets instead (p. 294). Here, however, he wishes to adopt his mother's point of view of Miriam's instinct for possession, which springs, as he tells her savagely, from a fundamental weakness: 'You don't want to love – your eternal and abnormal craving is to be loved. You aren't positive, you're negative. You absorb, absorb, as if you must fill yourself up with love, because you've got a shortage somewhere' (p. 274). However, once the scene is read in conjunction with the narrative point of view and the symbolism of the flowers, the daffodils are seen to have a very different function. The author's description of the cheeks of the daffodils as 'greenish with cold' slides almost imperceptibly into Miriam's own response to them, which is to caress their cold cheeks with her own warm ones. Her intoxication is not with possession, but with the magnificent otherness of the flowers, which she defines in contrast to her own humanity; while Paul stands condemned for his inability to be drawn, as the author clearly is, into the wonder of the flowers. And his verbal assault on Miriam elicits a severe comment from the authorial voice: 'She was stunned by his cruelty, and did not hear. He had not the faintest notion of what he was saying. It was as if his fretted, tortured soul, run hot by thwarted passion, jetted off these sayings like sparks from electricity' (p. 274).

Sympathy is preserved in some measure for Paul, who longs for the untaxing male companionship of Edgar (and diverts his attention to the bull terrier instead); by Miriam's pity for his vulnerability to the bitterness of life, for his childlike stupidity, and for the influence of his mother on his present state of mind. What the careful craftsmanship of this whole section of the novel – this return of Paul from Miriam to his mother – registers, then, is not the corrupting influence of Miriam's possessive love, but the profoundly Oedipal structure of the novel's central relationship, which is finally underlined by the conjunction of the points of view of Paul and his mother, bringing the completed episode to an ironic close: 'There was one place in the world that stood solid and did not melt into unreality: the place where his mother was. Everybody else could grow shadowy, almost non-existent to him, but she could not. It was as if the pivot and pole of his life, from which he could not escape, was his mother' (p. 278). And this is counterpointed by Mrs Morel's equally powerful, possessive love: 'Wherever he went she felt her soul went with him. Whatever he did she felt her soul stood by him, ready, as it were, to hand him his tools. She could not bear it when he was with Miriam. William was dead. She would fight to keep Paul' (ibid.).

Conclusion

In *Sons and Lovers* Lawrence is concerned above all to offer a subtle, balanced and truthful account of a highly complex reality, and he does so through the integration of the formal elements of drama and poetry, the achievement of an organic unity, and the maintenance of an almost clinical artistic impersonality. Although the carefully sustained equilibrium between sympathy and judgement is occasionally disturbed by authorial intrusions of the kind referred to earlier, when the narrator affirms that Morel had 'denied the God in him' (p. 102), or when we are informed that already, as he looks out of the window of the library reading-room, Paul was a 'prisoner of industrialism' (p. 131), such instances are rare, because this equipoise – this balanced view of every character, relationship and human situation – is an essential aspect of Lawrence's art. It is manifested in the superbly realistic ambivalence of the novel's conclusion, which is created by Lawrence's emphasis on the almost overwhelming complexity of Paul's final moral and instinctual choice.

Although critics such as Mark Schorer argue that Lawrence's closeness to his hero, resulting in an overlapping point of view, determines the inartistic wish fulfilment of an ending that he regards as optimistic, we have already observed how at points of crisis Lawrence distances himself from his hero; it is not at all surprising, therefore, to encounter a conclusion in which sympathy and judgement, optimism and pessimism, are in tension. Nor is it unexpected to find Paul torn almost equally between his contrary impulses towards death and life – between following his mother into the grave and returning to the world of his father. Throughout the novel, its profound Oedipal structure has been balanced by Paul's powerful emotional bond with the mining community, by his love for Miriam, by his relationship with Clara Dawes, by his friendship with the girls at Jordan's and his gregarious association with the socialist group in Nottingham (and by his approval of the commercial world into which his artistic talent is taking him) – which constitute a complementary structure of emotional relationships. Paul's choice is an agonising one. The ambiguous mercy killing of his mother effectively releases him from his dependence upon her, but he carries within him as a result a peculiarly profound knowledge of death. The driving-force of his life has gone, and the future is bleak. However, he retains the clenched will to endure, and he instinctively turns towards the community of the town, making for the world of the living, of work, and of his father's people: 'But no, he would not give in. Turning sharply, he walked towards the city's gold phosphorescence. His fists were shut, his mouth set fast. He would not take that direction, to the darkness, to follow her. He walked towards the faintly humming, glowing town, quickly' (p. 492). *Sons and Lovers* ends not, in Daniel Weiss's phrase, as a 'comedy of the Oedipus complex', nor as a tragedy in the strict sense, but in truthful ambiguity.

References

Source criticism

Chambers, Jessie, *D.H. Lawrence: A Personal Record*, by 'E.T.' (London, 1935), reissued with additional material by J.D. Chambers and others (London, 1965).

Gomme, A.H. (ed.), *D.H. Lawrence: A Critical Study of the Major Novels and Other Writings* (Sussex, 1978).

Hoffman, Frederick J., with Moore, Harry T., and others, *The Achievement of D.H. Lawrence* (Norman, Oklahoma, 1953).

Hough, Graham, *The Dark Sun: A Study of D.H. Lawrence* (London, 1956).

Moore, Harry T., *D.H. Lawrence: His Life and Works* (New York, 1950, rev. edn. 1964).

Worthen, John, *D.H. Lawrence and the Idea of the Novel* (London, 1979).

Psychoanalytical criticism

Kuttner, Alfred Booth, '*Sons and Lovers*: A Freudian Appreciation', *Psychoanalytic Review*, 3 (July 1916) pp. 295–317.

Murry, J. Middleton, *Son of Woman* (London, 1931).

O'Connor, Frank, *The Mirror in the Roadway* (London, 1955).

Weiss, Daniel A., *Oedipus in Nottingham: D.H. Lawrence* (Seattle, 1962).

Historical criticism

Holderness, Graham, *D.H. Lawrence: History, Ideology and Fiction* (London, 1982).

Lukács, Georg, *The Historical Novel* (London, 1962).

Sanders, Scott, *D.H. Lawrence: The World of the Major Novels* (London, 1973).
Williams, Raymond, *Marxism and Literature* (Oxford, 1974).

Feminist criticism

Beauvoir, Simone de, *The Second Sex* (London, 1953; French original, Paris, 1949).
Blanchard, Lydia, 'Love and Power: A Reconsideration of Sexual Politics in D.H. Lawrence', *Modern Fiction Studies*, 21 (1975) pp. 431–43.
Millett, Kate, *Sexual Politics* (New York, 1970; London, 1971).
Nin, Anaïs, *D.H. Lawrence: An Unprofessional Study* (Paris, 1932; London, 1961).
Pullin, Faith, 'Lawrence's Treatment of Women in *Sons and Lovers*', in *Lawrence and Women*, ed. Anne Smith (London, 1978).
Simpson, Hilary, *D.H. Lawrence and Feminism* (London, 1982).
Woolf, Virginia, *A Room of One's Own* (London, 1928).

Formalist criticism

Betsky, Seymour, 'Rhythm and Theme in *Sons and Lovers*', in Frederick J. Hoffman, Harry T. Moore and others, *The Achievement of D.H. Lawrence* (Norman, Oklahoma, 1953).
Hardy, Barbara, *The Appropriate Form* (London, 1964).
Leavis, F.R., *D.H. Lawrence: Novelist* (London, 1955).
Moynahan, Julian, *The Deed of Life: The Novels and Tales of D.H. Lawrence* (Princeton, 1963).
Sagar, Keith, *The Art of D.H. Lawrence* (Cambridge, 1966).
Schorer, Mark, 'Technique as Discovery', *Hudson Review*, 1 (Spring 1948), pp. 67–87.
Van Ghent, Dorothy, *The English Novel: Form and Function* (New York, 1953).

Genre criticism

Beebe, Maurice, *Ivory Towers and Sacred Founts* (New York, 1964).

Buckley, Jerome H., *Season of Youth: The Bildungsroman from Dickens to Golding* (Cambridge, Mass., 1974).

Other criticism

Daleski, H.M., *The Forked Flame: A Study of D.H. Lawrence* (London, 1965).
Draper, R.P., *D.H. Lawrence: The Critical Heritage* (London, 1969).
Eagleton, Terry, *Literary Theory: An Introduction* (Oxford, 1983).
Salgādo, Gāmini (ed.), *D.H. Lawrence: 'Sons and Lovers': A Casebook* (London, 1969).
Widdowson, Peter (ed.), *Re-reading English* (London, 1982).

Further reading

Dix, Carol, *D.H. Lawrence and Women* (London, 1980). A feminist view of the women characters in the novels.

Ford, George H., *Double Measure* (New York, 1965). Examines Lawrence's early writing in relation to his life.

Lerner, Laurence, *The Truthtellers* (London, 1967). Includes an account of the father figure in *Sons and Lovers*.

Moore, Harry T., *The Intelligent Heart* (London, 1955; rev. edn. 1960). A reliable biography, also available in Penguin paperback.

Nehls, Edward, *D.H. Lawrence: A Composite Biography*, 3 vols. (Madison, Wis. 1957–9). A collection of memoirs, autobiographical materials and letters, and the most important biographical work.

Roberts, Warren, and Moore, Harry T., *D.H. Lawrence and his World* (London, 1966). Introduces the background to *Sons and Lovers*.

Salgādo, Gāmini, *D.H. Lawrence: 'Sons and Lovers'* (London, 1966). A straightforward and sensitive reading of the novel.

Spilka, Mark, *The Love Ethic of D.H. Lawrence* (Bloomington, Ind., 1955; London, 1958). Includes a useful essay on Lawrence's treatment of love in *Sons and Lovers*.

Tedlock, E.W., (ed.), *D.H. Lawrence and 'Sons and Lovers': Sources and Criticism* (New York, 1965; London, 1966). Contains a good selection of essays, with a helpful introduction.

Vivas, Eliseo, *D.H. Lawrence: The Failure and the Triumph of Art* (Evanston, 1960; London, 1961). Discusses Lawrence's symbolism.

Index